HISTORY OF THE UNITED STATES

Drawn by Will H. Low.

The World's Fair at Chicago. Central Portion of MacMonnies Fountain—Effect
of Electric Light.

HISTORY OF
THE UNITED STATES

FROM THE EARLIEST DISCOVERY OF
AMERICA TO THE END OF 1902

BY

E. BENJAMIN ANDREWS

CHANCELLOR OF THE UNIVERSITY OF NEBRASKA
FORMERLY PRESIDENT OF BROWN UNIVERSITY

With 550 Illustrations and Maps

VOLUME IV.

NEW YORK
CHARLES SCRIBNER'S SONS
1904

CONTENTS

PERIOD IV

CIVIL WAR AND RECONSTRUCTION

(*Continued*)

1860–1868

Grant Lieutenant-General.—Plan of Campaign for 1864–65.
—Sherman's Army.—Skirmishes.—Kenesaw Mountain.—Johnston at Bay.—Hood in Command.—Assumes the Offensive.—Sherman in Atlanta.—Losses.—Hood to Alabama and Tennessee.—The March to the Sea.—Living on the Country.—Sherman at Savannah.—Hardee Evacuates.—A Christmas Gift.—The Blow to the Confederacy.—Thomas Crushes Hood.—Sherman Marches North.—Charleston Falls.—Columbia.—Johnston Routed at Bentonville.—Sherman Master of the Carolinas.—Johnston Surrenders.

McClellan to Fortress Monroe.—Yorktown.—Williamsburg.—Fair Oaks.—Lee in Command.—McDowell Retained at Fredericksburg.—Lee Assumes the Offensive.—Gaines's Mill.—The Seven Days' Retreat.—Malvern Hill.—Union Army at Harrison's Landing.—Discouragement.—McClellan Leaves the Peninsula.—Pope's Advance on Richmond.—Retreat.—Jackson in his Rear.—Second Battle of Bull Run.—Pope Defeated.—Chantilly.—McClellan again Commander.—Lee in Maryland.—South Mountain.—Antietam.—Lee Escapes.—McClellan Removed and Burnside in Command.—Fredericksburg.—The Battle. — Hooker General-in-Chief. — Chancellorsville. — Flank Movement by Jackson.—Battle of May 3d.—Lee in Pennsylvania.—Convergence to Gettysburg.—First Day's Battle.—Second Day.— Third.— Pickett's Charge.— Failure.— Lee Escapes.—Significance of this Battle.

Grant Comes East.—Battle of the Wilderness.—Flanking.—Spottsylvania.—The " Bloody Angle."—Butler " Bottled Up" at Bermuda.—Grant at the North Anna.—At Cold Harbor.—Change of Base to the James.—Siege of Petersburg.—The Mine.—Washington in Peril.—Operations in Shenandoah Valley.—" Sheridan's Ride."—Further Work at Petersburg.—Distress at the South.—Lee's Problem.—Battle at Five Forks.—Blue-coats in Petersburg.—Davis and his Government Leave Richmond.—

Union Army Enters.—Grant Pursues Lee.—The Surrender.—
Assassination of President Lincoln.—Johnston Grounds Arms.
—Capture of Jefferson Davis.

PERIOD V

THE CEMENTED UNION

1868–1888

LIST OF ILLUSTRATIONS

PAGE

LIST OF MAPS

PERIOD IV.

CIVIL WAR AND RECONSTRUCTION

(*Continued*)

1860–1868

CHAPTER V.

THE STRUGGLE FOR THE MISSISSIPPI VALLEY

THE North conducted the war upon three great lines of campaign: 1. The Western campaigns, to clear the Mississippi River and thus divide the Confederacy. 2. The campaigns in the centre, to reach the sea at Mobile, Savannah, or Charleston, cutting the Confederacy a second time. 3. The Eastern campaigns, to take Richmond, and capture or destroy the main Confederate army, ending the Confederacy. This chapter deals with the Western campaigns alone.

The opening of 1862 found the Confederates in possession of a strong line across the southern portion of Western Kentucky, stretching from Bowling Green, near the centre of the State, to Columbus

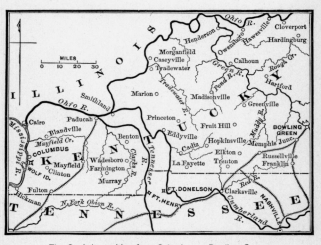

The Confederate Line from Columbus to Bowling Green.

on the Mississippi.   The two gates of this line were Forts Henry and Donelson, on the Tennessee and Cumberland Rivers, respectively, just over the Tennessee border.   If these forts could be taken the Confederates must give up Kentucky.

On February 6th, after a two hours'
bombardment, Fort Henry surrendered to

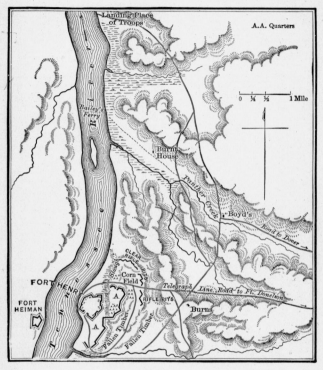

Fort Henry.

General Grant, who had come up the river
from Cairo with 17,000 troops, and with
seven gunboats commanded by Commodore

Foote. Most of the garrison, about 3,000, had been sent off before the fleet opened fire, General Tilghman foreseeing that he could not hold the fort. The land forces arrived too late to cut off their retreat, and they escaped safely to Fort Donelson, some dozen miles to the east.

Grant marched at once to invest Donelson, and sat down before it on the 12th with 15,000 men. The stronghold stood upon a bluff 100 feet high. On the east it was protected by the Cumberland River; on the north and south by two flooded creeks. Along a crest back of the fort a mile or two ran a semicircular line of rifle-pits, with abatis in front. Nine batteries were posted at various points along the line. Donelson was garrisoned by 20,000 men under Generals Floyd, Pillow, and Buckner, who quietly looked on while Grant's smaller army hemmed them in. On the 14th the gunboats opened fire upon the water batteries between fort and river. Commodore Foote steamed up boldly within 400 yards and pounded the oppos-

ing works with his heavy guns. He did
little damage, however, while the Confederate fire proved very effective against him.
His flag-ship, the Hartford, was struck fifty-
nine times. A shot crashed into the pilot-
house, destroying the wheel and wounding

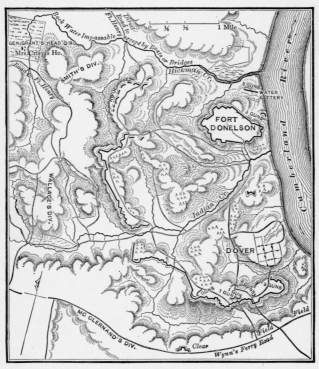

Fort Donelson.

Foote himself. The boat became unmanageable and drifted down-stream. A shot cut the tiller-ropes of the Louisville. The other boats were also considerably damaged, and after an action of an hour and a half, the entire fleet withdrew.

But Grant's army had been re-enforced to 27,000. Three divisions, under Smith, Wallace, and McClernand, stretched in a semicircle about Donelson from north to south. On the night of the 14th the Confederate generals held a consultation, and decided to try cutting their way out. Most of the troops were withdrawn from the rifle-pits during the night, and massed on the Union right. The weather had suddenly turned frosty, and the Union men, without tents or camp-fires, many even without blankets, shivered all night in the intense cold. Before dawn the attacking column from inside, 10,000 strong, rushed through the woods and fell upon McClernand's division, which formed the Union right. For hours the woods rang with musketry and the southern yell. Slowly the Con-

federates drove the Unionists before them
and gained the road running south to Char-
lotte, opening to themselves the way of
escape.

This, however, they had not yet utilized,
when, about one o'clock, General Grant,
who had been aboard the fleet consulting
with Commodore Foote, came upon the
field. Learning that the foe had begun
to fight with full haversacks, he instantly
divined that they were trying to make
their escape, and inferred that their forces
had been mostly withdrawn from opposite
the Union left to make this attack against
the right. General Smith was therefore
instantly ordered to fall upon the Confederate right. As Grant had surmised, the
intrenchments there were easily carried.
Meanwhile the demoralized soldiers of the
Union right and centre rallied, and drove
the Confederates back to their intrenchments. At daybreak Buckner sent to
Grant for terms of capitulation. " No
terms except unconditional and immediate
surrender can be accepted : I propose to

move immediately upon your works," was
the answer. The resolute words rang
through the North, carrying big hope in
their remotest echo. Donelson surrendered. Floyd and Pillow had sneaked

General John Pope

away during the night, the former monop-
olizing the few boats to transport his
own brigade. Fifteen thousand troops remained and were taken prisoners.

The capture of Henry and Donelson
necessitated the evacuation of Bowling
Green and Columbus. Kentucky was now

clear of Confederates, and the Mississippi
open down to Island Number Ten. This
island lay in a bend of the river at the
extreme northwestern corner of Tennessee.
The great stream here runs northwest for
a dozen miles, then sharply turns to the
south again. New Madrid stands at this
northern bend. It was protected by Confederate fortifications and gunboats. Early
in March, General Halleck, now at the
head of the Western Department, sent
General Pope against New Madrid with
20,000 men. The enemy fled to Island
Number Ten, leaving thirty-three guns,
besides ammunition and many tents.

Island Number Ten was strongly fortified. Commodore Foote came down the
river with seventeen gunboats, and on
March 16th began a bombardment which
was kept up for three weeks with little
effect; but early in April Pope got upon
the Tennessee shore, in the undefended
rear of the island, and by intercepting its
communication to the south, forced it to
surrender, April 8th. Seven thousand

prisoners, one hundred heavy siege guns, several thousand small arms, besides large stores of ammunition and supplies, were thus secured, without the loss of a single Union soldier. This exploit brought to Pope great fame.

Pope now descended the river to Fort Pillow, 100 miles below, which he prepared to take. He was just then transferred by Halleck to another field, and the reduction of Pillow left to the gunboats. Pillow was abandoned June 4th. The Union flotilla, increased by four rams, now ran down the river to Memphis, where, on June 6th, in the presence of thousands of spectators upon the bluffs, it fought a battle with a southern fleet. Seven of the Confederate boats were destroyed, and the next day Memphis surrendered.

After the fall of Donelson the Confederates began concentrating their forces at Corinth, in the northeast corner of Mississippi. Meanwhile the Army of the Tennessee, under orders from Halleck, had moved up the Tennessee River, and en-

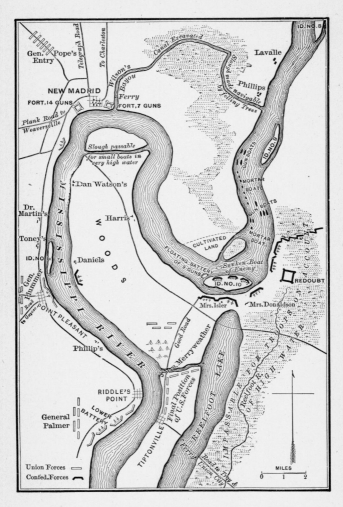

New Madrid and Island Number Ten.

camped, some 40,000 strong, at Pittsburg
Landing on the Tennessee River, 25 miles
north of Corinth.   Here Grant, who had
been temporarily removed, took command
again on March 17th.   Buell, with 40,000
men, was on the march thither from Central Tennessee.   The Confederate generals
at Corinth, Albert Sidney Johnston and
Beauregard, wisely determined to strike
Grant before Buell arrived.   There ensued
the greatest battle[1] which had up to that
time shaken the solid ground of this continent.

About six o'clock on the morning of
April 6th the Confederates burst through
the thick woods upon the Union pickets
and drove them in.   It was at least partially a surprise.   Grant in person was nine
miles down the river.   The Union officers
hastily got their men into line, as the attacking columns came sweeping in after the
pickets.   Three of the five Union divisions
were raw recruits, many of whom fled at

---

[1] Indifferently called the battle of Shiloh or the battle of Pittsburg Landing.

the first fire. Some colonels led their entire regiments off the field. Later in the
day Grant saw 4,000 or 5,000 of these run-
aways cowering under the shelter of the
bluffs.

General William T. Sherman.

But the bulk of the army made a stub-
born resistance. General W. T. Sherman,
then comparatively unknown, inspired his
division of raw troops with his own intelligent courage. Their gallant and pro-

tracted fight around the Shiloh log church made them the heroes of the day. But the Confederates' onset was impetuous. Step by step they forced their opponents back through the heavy woods, and by noon stood in possession of the Union camps; Grant's army, badly shattered, being cooped up in a narrow space along the edge of the river.

The tide now turned. About two o'clock, General Johnston was killed, and the Confederate advance flagged. Between the two armies lay a deep ravine. Grant planted some fifty guns upon the edge, and two of the gunboats took positions where they could rake the ravine. By these dispositions Beauregard's advance was stayed. Night fell, and hostilities ceased.

Fortunately, 22,000 of Buell's men arrived during the night, and next morning Grant ordered an advance. Beauregard made as desperate a resistance as he could, seeing that his heavy losses the day before had left him but 30,000 troops fit for duty.

A.R.WARD

H.B.HALL,JR.

The Battle of the Rams at Memphis, June 6, 1862.

Buell's men showed the effects of long train-
ing under that matchless disciplinarian, and
fought splendidly.   The enemy were steadily pushed back, until more than all the
ground lost on the preceding day had been
triumphantly regained, and the battle of
Pittsburg Landing, from being for the
Union side a defeat accomplished and
a surrender threatened, was turned into a
bright and inspiring victory.   Beauregard
ordered a retreat, and, not being pursued,
regained his old position at Corinth.   He
had lost about 10,000 men.   Our loss was
12,000, including four regiments taken prisoners.   The battle was a severe check to
both sides.

On February 2d the largest fleet that had
ever sailed under the American flag left
Fortress Monroe for the mouth of the
Mississippi, commanded by Commodore
Farragut.   It consisted of 16 gunboats,
21 mortar-schooners, six sloops of war, and
five other vessels.   Fifteen thousand land
troops, under General Butler, soon followed.   Thirty miles below New Orleans

Forts Jackson and St. Philip, mounting 100 guns, frowned at each other across the Mississippi. Farragut's fleet sailed up the river and the mortar-schooners were moored to the banks within range of the forts.

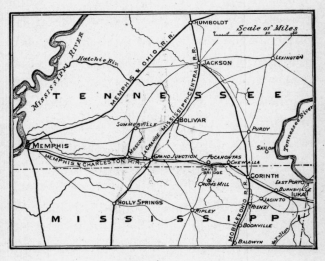

Memphis to Iuka. 1862.

Boughs were tied to the top-masts so that the enemy could not distinguish them from the trees along the shore. April 18th the mortars began shelling the forts. An incessant fire was kept up night and day, for six days, till nearly 6,000 shells had been thrown.

As the forts sustained little damage, Farragut decided to run the batteries. A gunboat stole up by night and cut the boom of hulks chained together, which crossed the river just below the forts. Some of the boats were rubbed over with mud to make them invisible, and chain cables hung over the sides to protect the engines. About half past two in the night of April 23d the fleet moved up the river through the gap in the boom. The enemy, on the alert, launched fire-rafts and lit bon-fires to lift the cover of night. Old Jackson and St. Philip poured a hot fire into the fleet as vessel after vessel slowly steamed past, answering with its most spiteful broadsides.

But the Union craft had more than the forts against them. Once past the boom they were in the midst of a hostile fleet of fifteen vessels, including a dangerous iron-clad ram. A fierce water-fight followed. The Union Varuna was sunk ; the flag-ship

Hartford set on fire by one of the fire-rafts.
The flames, however, were soon put out.
Other vessels were disabled.   But every
one of the Confederate ships was captured
or destroyed, and Jackson and St. Philip
had to surrender.   Farragut then sailed
up the river and took possession of New
Orleans without resistance.   Butler at once
occupied the city with his troops, and the
Stars and Stripes again waved over the
Crescent City.   Since that eventful day
New Orleans has never been in disunionist
hands.

After the battle of Pittsburg Landing,
Halleck himself came down from St. Louis,
and took the reins.   Grant was nominally
in command under him, but had next
to nothing to do.   Re-enforced by 25,000
men under Pope, Halleck slowly advanced
toward Corinth, entering the place May
30th, Beauregard having evacuated it May
29th.   A few Quaker guns—logs mounted
on wagon-wheels—were the only trophies.
Halleck now had 110,000 effectives, Beauregard less than 60,000.   Halleck lay in-

Farragut in the Main-Rigging.

From the original by William Page.

active at Corinth for six weeks, when he
was summoned to Washington as General-
in-Chief.

Grant once more took command of the
forces about Corinth, which re-enforcements
to Eastern Tennessee soon reduced to 42,-
000. With these he was expected to guard
200 miles of railroad, from Memphis to
Decatur in Northern Alabama. The Confederates under Van Dorn and Price attempted to regain Corinth, but in the
battles of Iuka, September 19th, and Corinth, October 3d and 4th, were repulsed
with heavy losses. Grant then took the
offensive. Vicksburg, about half-way from
north to south on Mississippi's western
boundary, was the only stronghold left to
the Confederates on the great river. Its
capture would ideally complete the western campaign. Grant's plan was for Sherman to descend the river from Memphis,
while he himself simultaneously attacked
Vicksburg by land.

So long as the stout-hearted general continued his march south all his supplies had

to be brought over the Mississippi Central Railroad from Holly Springs, near the Tennessee border. A troop of 3,500 Confederate cavalry, making a long detour around

General Henry W. Halleck.

his army, swooped down upon Holly Springs, December 20th, captured the garrison of 1,300 men, and destroyed all the stores, valued at $2,000,000. For two weeks the Union army had to live from the enemy's country, and then after all to

fall back to Holly Springs.   Meanwhile
Sherman, ignorant of his superior's ill fortune, descended the Mississippi, and with a
force of 30,000 made during the last days
of the year an unsuccessful attack upon
Vicksburg.

Very early in January, 1863, McClernand
arrived near Vicksburg with re-enforcements.   The last of the month, Grant,
who had given up the land expedition,
took command in person.   Sherman's repulse had shown that Vicksburg could
not be taken from the water side.   A
position must be gained in the rear.   This
seemed, and indeed proved, an almost impossible task.   The Mississippi was unusu-
ally high, and the surrounding country a
vast network of bayous and swamps.   The
winter passed away in fruitless labors to
make some sort of a water passage to the
rear of Vicksburg, either above, via the
Yazoo, or around through Louisiana to
some point below the city, whence the
army could cross again to the Vicksburg
side of the Mississippi and strike Pem-

berton's stronghold from the southeast. In most of these attempts Grant himself had little faith, but the army was better at work than idle. At last he resolved, without attempting a regular canal, partly by land but utilizing bayous and creeks as he could, to swing his army across west of the river to New Carthage, south of Vicksburg, run the Vicksburg batteries with the fleet, and, uniting his land and water forces in the capture of Grand Gulf, to gain the rear of Vicksburg by way of the Big Black River. It was a bold plan, but it succeeded.

In April, by building corduroy roads through miles of swamp and bridging numberless bayous, the general succeeded in reaching New Carthage, some twenty miles south of Vicksburg, with a good part of his land forces. On the night of April 16th, the gunboats and provision transports ran the gauntlet of Vicksburg's guns with little damage. The last of the month a landing was effected just below Grand Gulf, on the east bank, fifteen or twenty miles still farther south of Vicksburg. The enemy made some resistance, but were driven back.

Grant's position was now full of peril. He was in the heart of the enemy's country. Pemberton was occupying Jackson and Vicksburg with 50,000 men. General Joseph E. Johnston was hurrying to his aid with re-enforcements. Grant's forces available for an advance about equalled Pemberton's. A bold policy was the only safe one. Taking five days' rations, he cut loose from his base at Grand Gulf and marched north to attack Pemberton before Johnston could join him. Jackson, forty-four miles to the east of Vicksburg, was easily captured, May 14th. Grant had thus thrust himself in between Johnston and Pemberton. Turning to the left he smote Pemberton a heavy blow at Champion's Hill on the 16th, and drove him into Vicksburg. Johnston fell back baffled. In eighteen days Grant had marched 200 miles, defeated the enemy in four engagements, inflicting a loss of 8,000 and taking 88 guns, and shut up a large

army in Vicksburg—all this upon five days'
rations.   It is a brilliant record, equalled,
if at all, only by some of Napoleon's campaigns.

Operations in Louisiana. February to July, 1863.

The bold commander now transferred his
base of supplies to the Yazoo River, which
runs into the Mississippi a few miles above
Vicksburg.   After an unsuccessful assault

upon the city's strong intrenchments, he sat
down to a deliberate siege. Twelve miles
of trenches were constructed. Eighty-nine
batteries, with more than 200 guns, day after
day rained shot and shell against the Vicksburg fortifications. The lines of investment
crept nearer and nearer the fated city. The
pickets chaffed with each other, and exchanged tobacco and newspapers. June
25th, a mine was exploded under one of the
Vicksburg parapets, but it made no effec-
tual breach. A second explosion, July 1st,
was equally unavailing. Johnston kept
menacing the rear, but feared to attack, as
Grant had been re-enforced to 60,000.

Famine began to threaten the city, Porter's fleet blockading the water front.
Flour sold for $1,000 a barrel in Confed-
erate money. Mule flesh became the chief
meat. Rats were hung up for sale in the
market. The inhabitants sought protection
from the shells in cellars and caves. Cave-
digging became a regular business. The
Vicksburg daily news sheet was now printed
on wall paper. July 3d, white flags ap-

peared upon the city's works.   An armistice followed, and the next day Pemberton surrendered.   The prisoners, some 30,000 in number, were mostly released on parole. With the fall of Vicksburg the western campaigns virtually closed.   The capture of Port Hudson, below, was assured from that moment, and followed on July 8th. The " Father of Waters " once more rolled " unvexed to the sea," and the Confederacy was cut in twain.

CHAPTER VI.

THE WAR IN THE CENTRE

WE have seen that the fall of Donelson had driven the Confederates out of Kentucky. In the following September, 1862, Bragg invaded the State from Tennessee with 40,000 men. Buell hurried north from Nashville, and after an exciting race headed him off from Louisville. Bragg slowly fell back, first east, then south. Kentucky was rich in food and clothing, and his army plundered freely, coming out, it was boasted, with a wagon-train forty miles long. At Perryville Bragg turned upon Buell fiercely. An indecisive battle was fought, October 8, 1862, which gave the richly loaded wagon-train time to escape into Tennessee, whither Bragg followed.

The Christmas holidays of 1862 found the Confederate host at Murfreesboro,

Tenn., thirty miles southeast of Nashville, where the Union army lay. Rosecrans, who had succeeded Buell, moved suddenly to the banks of Stone River, within four miles of the gay town, and prepared to attack. Bragg, like Wellington from Brussels on the morning of Waterloo, hurried forth to meet him. At dawn, December 31st, the gray-colored columns emerged from the fog that overhung the river, and spiritedly beat up the Union right. Two divisions were swept back. Sheridan's men, inspired by their dashing leader, held their ground for awhile, but fell rearward at last; and, forming a new line, stood at bay with fixed bayonets. Rosecrans recalled the troops who had crossed the river to make a similar attack upon the Confederate right, and massed all his forces at the point of assault. Six times the southrons charged, six times they were tumbled back by the Union batteries double-shotted with canister. Night fell on a drawn battle.

The next day, January 1, 1863, was

peaceful save for cavalry skirmishing. January 2d the awful combat was renewed. Rosecrans having planted artillery upon commanding ground, Bragg must either carry this or fall back. He attempted the

General William S. Rosecrans.

first alternative, and was repulsed with terrible slaughter, losing 2,000 men in forty minutes. He escaped south under cover of a storm. In proportion to the numbers engaged, the battle of Stone River was one of the bloodiest in the war. About 45,000 fought on each side. The Union loss was 12,000, the Confederate nearly 15,000.

Rosecrans did not advance again till June, although Bragg lay quite near. The latter fell back as the Unionists approached, first into Chattanooga and then over the Georgia line. Rosecrans followed. Bragg was now re-enforced, and determined to retake Chattanooga, which lay on the Tennessee River and was an important strategical point. The two armies met on Chickamauga Creek, twelve miles south of Chattanooga. All through the first day's battle, September 19th, there was hot fighting—charges and countercharges—but no decisive advantage fell to either side. During the night Bragg was re-enforced by Longstreet's corps from Virginia, and he opened the next day's fight with an assault upon the Union left. Brigades were moved from the centre to support the left. Through the gap thus made Longstreet poured his men in heavy columns, cutting the Union army in two. Its right wing became demoralized, and

fled toward Chattanooga in wild confusion,
Rosecrans after it at a gallop, believing
that all was lost.

But all was not lost. General Thomas
commanded the Union left. Like a flinty
rock he stood while Polk's and Longstreet's
troops surged in heavy masses against his
front and flank. About three o'clock heavy
columns were seen pouring through a gorge
almost in Thomas's rear. They were Longstreet's men. It was a critical moment.
Granger's reserves came rushing upon the
field. Raw recruits though they were, they
dashed against Longstreet like veterans.
In twenty minutes, at cost of frightful
slaughter, the gorge and ridge were theirs.
Longstreet made another assault, but was
again repulsed. At nightfall Thomas fell
back to Chattanooga, henceforth named,
and justly, the "Rock of Chickamauga."
For six hours he had held his own with
25,000 braves against twice that number.
Out of 70,000 troops Bragg lost probably
20,000. Rosecrans's force was about 55,000,
his loss 16,000.

Bragg proceeded to shut up the Union army in Chattanooga. Grant, now commanding the Department of the Mississippi, was ordered to recover Chattanooga,

General George H. Thomas.

and his deeds along this front, though less often mentioned, will glitter upon the page of history with little if any less lustre than those about Vicksburg. Upon his arrival, late in October, he found the city practically in a state of siege. Its railroad communication with Nashville was cut off, and supplies had to be hauled in wagons sixty miles over a rough mountain road. The men had been for some time on half rations. Thousands of horses and mules had starved, and the artillery could not be moved for lack of teams. There was not ammunition enough for one day's fighting. In five days Grant wrested the railroad from Bragg's men and bridged the Tennessee, so that an abundant supply of food and ammunition came pouring in.

Elated at his Chickamauga triumph, and unaware that he now had a greater than Rosecrans in his front, Bragg deemed it a safe and promising stratagem to despatch Longstreet's corps to Knoxville to capture Burnside. It was a fatal step, and Grant was not slow to take advantage of it. He telegraphed Sherman to put his entire force instantly *en route* from Vicksburg to Chattanooga.

Chattanooga lies on the south side of the Tennessee River, at the northern end of a valley running north and south. Along the eastern edge of the valley rises Missionary Ridge. On the western side and farther south, stands Lookout Mountain. After passing Chattanooga, the river turns and runs south till it laves the base of Lookout Mountain. The Confederate fortifications, twelve miles in length, ran along Missionary Ridge, across the southern end of the valley, and up over Lookout Mountain.

On November 23d, Thomas, who had succeeded Rosecrans, stormed the breastworks half a mile from the base of Missionary Ridge. The next day Grant sent "Fighting Joe Hooker" to sweep Bragg's detachment from Lookout Mountain. Mist lay along the lofty slopes as the gallant Hooker and his men moved up them, soon veiling the entire column from sight; and it was only by the rattle of the musketry that Grant knew how the fight progressed. This was the famous "Battle Above the Clouds." Hooker pounded the enemy so lustily that they were glad to evacuate the mountain in the night, and the next morning the Stars and Stripes saluted the breezes of its topmost peak.

While Hooker had been thus engaged, and for some days before, Sherman had

General Joseph Hooker.

been at a movement that was even more momentous. He had slyly thrust his army up the Tennessee River above the city, placing it between the river and Missionary Ridge, and had worked its flank to the left as far as the mouth of Chickamauga Creek.

He had thus gotten possession of the entire northeastern spur of that ridge with hardly the loss of a corporal's guard.

The morrow after this was accomplished, November 25, 1863, was a day of blood. Bragg's forces were now massed on Missionary Ridge, mainly in front of Thomas and Sherman. Hooker had come down into the valley and was to turn the enemy's left. If Bragg massed troops on either of the two wings, Thomas's braves were to be let slip against the weakened centre. Sherman got into action early in the morning, and fought his painfully difficult way slowly up the rugged acclivities in his front. Hooker had to bridge Chattanooga Creek, and did not attack till afternoon. By three o'clock Sherman was so hard pressed that Grant found it necessary to relieve him by sending Thomas forward at the centre.

The signal guns boom—one, two, three, four, five, six. Up spring Thomas's heroes from their breastworks, and rush like a whirlwind for the first line of Confederate rifle-pits. Bragg sees the advance and hur-

A. R. WAUD

H. B. HALL, Jr.

The Battle of Lookout Mountain. (The "Battle Above the Clouds.")

ries help to oppose.   His batteries open
with shot and shell, then with canister.
The infantry rake Thomas with a withering
fire.   Yet on, double quick, dash the lines
of blue over the open plain, over rocks,
stumps, and breastworks, bayonetting back
or capturing their antagonists, till the first
line of rifle-pits is theirs.

The orders had been to halt at this point
and re-form.   But here, with Bragg's artillery raining a veritable hell-fire upon them
—here is no place of resting, and as the
men's blood is up, they sweep forward un-
bidden, with a cheer.   It is five hundred
yards to the top—a steep ascent, covered
with bowlders and fallen timber.   Over the
rocks, under and through the timber, each
one scrambles on as he can.   Half-way up
is a line of small works.   It is carried
with a rush, and on the men go, right up
to the crest of the ridge.   Now they con-
front the heaviest breastworks.   The air is
thick with whizzing musket-balls, and fifty
cannon belch flame and death.   But nothing
can stop that furious charge.   Sheridan's

men reach the top first, the rest of the line close behind. The "Johnnies" are routed after a short fight, and the guns turned against them as they fly. By night Bragg's army is in full retreat, Chattanooga is safe

General James B. McPherson.

and free, Grant's lines of communication are assured, and the keys of the State of Georgia in his hands.

The Union forces in this battle numbered about 60,000, the Confederate half as many; but the latter fought with all the advantage which the mountain and breastworks could give them. They lost nearly 10,000, including 6,500 prisoners. The Union loss was between 5,000 and 6,000—2,200 in the one hour's charge against the centre.

There was no halting, no resting. Scarcely had the sounds of yesterday's cannonade died away, when Sherman's already jaded forces were put in motion to the north, to make sure that Burnside was set free at Knoxville; but Longstreet had already raised the siege and started east. By December 6th, Bragg's redoubtable army, which, so recently as September, swore to reconquer Tennessee and to invade Kentucky, was rent in twain, one part of it fleeing to Virginia, the other to the heart of Georgia.

No important military movement occurred in the Centre during this winter of 1863–64. In March Grant was made Lieutenant-General, with command of all the Union armies, Sherman succeeding to the headship of the Mississippi Department. The latter accompanied his superior toward Washington as far as Cincinnati, and there, in a parlor of the Burnet House, the two victorious generals, bending over their maps together, planned in outline that gigantic campaign of 1864–65, which was to end the war; then, grasping one another warmly by the hand, they parted, one starting east, the other south, each to strike at the appointed time his half of the ponderous death-blow.

Sherman pushed out from Chattanooga May 6, 1864, with 100,000 men and 254 cannon. His force comprised the Army of the Cumberland, 60,000, under Thomas; the Army of the Tennessee, 25,000, under Schofield; and the Army of the Ohio, 15,-000, under McPherson. Johnston, who had superseded Bragg, lay behind strong works at Dalton, a few miles southeast, with 64,000 men, his base being Atlanta, 80 miles away. Sherman's supplies all came over a single line of railroad from Nashville, nearly 150 miles from Chattanooga as the road ran. Every advantage but numbers was on Johnston's side.

Sherman calculated that the Army of the

Cumberland could hold his opponent at bay, while the two smaller armies crept around his flanks. This plan was adhered to throughout, and with wonderful success. All through May and the first of June a series of skilful flanking movements compelled Johnston to fall back from one position to another, each commander, like a tried boxer, constantly on the watch to catch his opponent off guard. Heavy skirmishing day after day made the march practically one long battle.

June 10th Johnston planted his army upon three elevations — Kenesaw, Pine, and Lost Mountains—and stubbornly stood at bay. A pouring rain, which turned the whole country into a quagmire and the streams into formidable rivers, made the usual flank manœuvre impracticable. Sherman resolved to assault in front. June 27th a determined onset was made along the whole line for two hours, but failed, though the troops gained positions close to the hostile works and intrenched. They lost 2,500 ; the Confederates not more than a third of this number.   The roads having now improved, Sherman resorted to his old tactics, the Confederates having to fall back across the Chattahoochee, and come to bay under the very guns of Atlanta.

Just at the critical moment, when Sherman's army was slowly closing in around Atlanta, General Johnston, so wary and cool, was superseded by the young and fiery Hood, pledged to assume the offensive.   On the 20th Hood made a furious attack on Hooker's front, but was repulsed with heavy losses.   On the 22d he struck again, and harder.   By a night march, Hardee's corps at dawn fell upon the Union left flank and rear like a thunderbolt out of a clear sky, rolling up the Army of the Tennessee in great confusion.   The brave and talented McPherson was killed early in the action, Logan succeeding. "McPherson and revenge," he cried, as upon his coal-black steed he careered from post to post of danger, inspiring his men and restoring order.   The veterans soon recovered from their surprise.   The Union

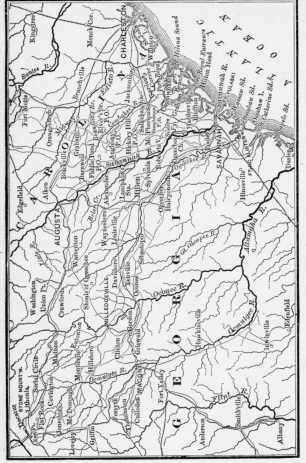

Atlanta to Savannah.

lines were completely re-established, and by night Hood's army was driven back into the city, having sacrificed probably 10,000 much-needed men, 2,500 of them killed.

Sherman now began to swing round to the south and southeast of Atlanta, till at last he cut its communications with the Confederacy. Hood evacuated the city and his opponent entered it, September 5th. The northern troops, after their four months' incessant marching and fighting, now got a little well-earned rest. Their total losses from Chattanooga were 32,000. The Confederates had sacrificed about 35,-000—the larger part under Hood.

The last of September Hood struck out boldly for Tennessee, menacing, and, in fact, temporarily rupturing Sherman's long supply-line from Nashville. Leaving one corps to hold Atlanta, Sherman raced back for 100 miles in pursuit. The railroad being well guarded, Hood could do no serious damage, and finally turned west into Alabama. Sherman now resolved on a march to the sea. Thomas, with three

corps, was sent to Tennessee to look out
for Hood. The 62,000 troops remaining
at Atlanta were put into light marching
trim, and the wagons filled with 20 days'
rations and 200 rounds of ammunition per
man. All storehouses and other property
useful to the enemy were then destroyed,
communications with the North cut, and
November 15th a splendid army of hardy
veterans swung off for the Atlantic or the
Gulf, over 200 miles away. Their orders
were to live on the country, the rations
being kept for emergencies; but no dwell-
ings were to be entered, and no houses or
mills destroyed if the army was unmolested.
The dwelling-house prescription was, alas,
too often broken over. There was little
resistance, Georgia having been drained of
its able-bodied whites. Negroes flocked,
singly and by families, to join "Massa
Linkum's boys." The railroads were destroyed, and the Carolinas thus cut off
from the Gulf States.

Each regiment detailed a certain number
of foragers. These, starting off in the

morning empty-handed and on foot, would return at night riding or driving beasts laden with spoils. "Here would be a silver-mounted family carriage drawn by a jackass and a cow, loaded inside and out with everything the country produced, vegetable and animal, dead and alive. There would be an ox-cart, similarly loaded, and drawn by a nondescript tandem team equally incongruous. Perched upon the top would be a ragged forager, rigged out in a fur hat of a fashion worn by dandies of a century ago, or a dress-coat which had done service at stylish balls of a former generation. The jibes and jeers, the fun and the practical jokes, ran down the whole line as the *cortége* came in, and no masquerade in carnival could compare with it for original humor and rollicking enjoyment. . . . The camps in the open pine-woods, the bon-fires along the railways, the occasional sham battles at night with blazing pine-knots for weapons whirling in the darkness, all combined to leave upon the minds of officers and men the impression of a vast holiday frolic." [1]

At the start Sherman was uncertain just where he should strike the coast. The blockade vessels were asked to be on the lookout for him from Mobile to Charleston. By the middle of December the army lay before Savannah. Hardee held the city with 16,000 men, but evacuated it December 20, 1864, Sherman entering next day. He wrote to Lincoln, "I beg to present you as a Christmas gift the city of Savannah." The capture of Fort McAllister a week before had opened the Ogeechee River, and Sherman now established a new base of supplies on the sea-coast.

The North rang with praises of the Great March, which had pierced like a knife the vitals of the Confederacy. Georgia, with her arsenals and factories, had been the Confederacy's workshop. Twenty thousand bales of cotton had been burned upon the march, besides a great amount

[1] *The March to the Sea*, by Major-General J. D. Cox. Campaigns of the Civil War. Scribners.

of military stores. The 320 miles of railroad destroyed had practically isolated Virginia from the South and the West. And all this had been done with the loss of less than 1,000 men.

Meanwhile Thomas had dealt the Confederacy another staggering blow. The adventurous Hood had advanced with his army of 44,000 to the very gates of Nashville. The deliberate Thomas, spite of prickings from Grant, waited till he felt prepared. Then he struck with a Titan's hand. The first day's fight, December 15th, drove the Confederate line back two miles. Hood formed again on hills running east and west, and hastily fortified. All next day the battle raged. Late in the afternoon the works on the Confederate left were carried by a gallant charge. Total rout of Hood's brave army followed. It fled south, demoralized and scattered, never to appear again as an organized force. In the two days' battle, 4,500 prisoners and 53 guns were taken.

February 1, 1865, his troops all rested

and equipped afresh, Sherman set his face
to the north.   The days of frolic were over.
Continuous rains had made the Carolinas

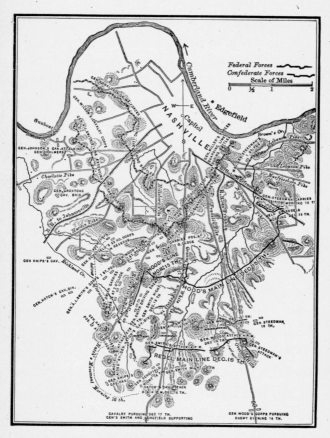

The Battle-Field of Nashville.

almost impassable. The march now begun was an incessant struggle with mud, swamps, and swollen rivers. A pontoon and trestle bridge three miles long was thrown across the Savannah, and miles of corduroy road were built through continuous swamps. Charleston, incessantly besieged since the war opened, where the United States had wasted more powder and iron than at all other points together, fell without a blow. Columbia was reached the middle of the month. It caught fire —just how has never been settled—and the greater part of the city was destroyed. Sherman's men helped to put out the flames, and left behind provisions and a herd of five hundred cattle for the suffering inhabitants.

The army pushed on toward North Carolina, destroying railroads as it went. Johnston was athwart their path with 30,000 men. March 16th he struck Sherman's army at Averysboro', N. C., and three days later at Bentonville. In the latter battle he was completely routed, and re-

treated during the night.   Sherman swept
on to Goldsboro', where re-enforcements

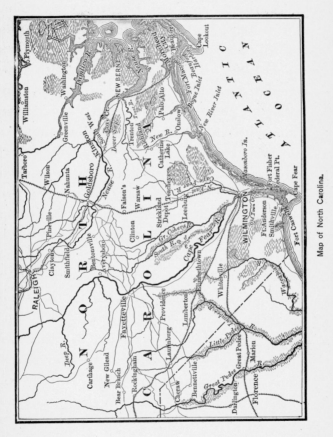

Map of North Carolina.

from the coast, under Schofield, increased
his army to 90,000.   He was undisputed

master of the Carolinas.   By this time
the Confederacy was hastening to its fall.
April 11th the news of Lee's surrender
was hailed in Sherman's army with shouts
of joy. A few days later Johnston surrendered to the hero of Atlanta and of
the March to the Sea.

CHAPTER VII.

THE VIRGINIA CAMPAIGNS OF 1862–63

THE Army of the Potomac lay inactive all through the winter of 1861–62. The country cried "Forward," but it was March before McClellan was ready to stir. Then he sailed down Chesapeake Bay to attack Richmond from the south, with Fortress Monroe as base. The splendidly disciplined and equipped army, 120,000 strong, began embarking March 17th.

Fortress Monroe lies at the apex of a wedge-shaped peninsula formed by the York and James Rivers, which converge as they flow toward the coast. April 4th, McClellan started on his march up this peninsula. A line of Confederate fortifications, twelve miles long, stretched across it, from Yorktown to the James, defended by 10,000 men. Yorktown must be taken to turn this line. A month was wasted in laborious siege preparations, for early in May, just before an overwhelming cannonade was to begin, the southern army evacu-

General David D. Porter.

ated the place and retreated toward Richmond.

McClellan hurried after it. A desultory battle was fought all day on the 5th, near Williamsburg, the enemy withdrawing at night. McClellan now moved slowly up the peninsula, the last of May finding his army within ten miles of Richmond, encamped on both sides of the Chickahominy. By this time nearly 70,000 troops had gathered for the defence of the Confederate capital.

General Robert E. Lee.

May 31st, the Confederate General Joseph E. Johnston fell upon the part of Mc-Clellan's army south of the river, at Fair Oaks, and in a bloody battle drove it back a mile. McClellan sent re-enforcements across the river, and the retreat was stayed. The lost ground was regained next day, and the enemy driven into Richmond. Johnston having been wounded, General Robert E. Lee was now placed in command of the Army of Virginia, destined to lay it down only at the collapse of the Confederate government.

McClellan waited three weeks for better weather. He also expected McDowell's corps of 45,000, which had been kept near Fredericksburg to defend Washington, but was under orders at the proper time to co-operate with McClellan by moving against Richmond from the north. But Stonewall Jackson came raiding down the Shenandoah Valley, hustling General Banks before him. Washington was alarmed, and McDowell had to be retained.

Lee boldly took the offensive, and the "Seven Days' Fight" began. June 26th he attacked McClellan's extreme right under Porter, on the north side of the Chickahominy. He was repulsed, but Porter fell back farther down the river to

Gaines's Mill, there fought all the next day against great odds, and was saved from total rout toward night only by the arrival of re-enforcements.

Jackson's army from the north had joined

General Nathaniel P. Banks.

Lee's left, and McClellan's communication with York River was in danger. He decided to change his base to the James, where he would have placed it at first but for his expectation of McDowell and his desire to connect with him. Everything not transportable, including millions of rations and hundreds of tons of ammunition, had to be destroyed. Five thousand loaded wagons, 2,500 head of cattle, and the reserve artillery were then set in motion toward the James, protected by the army in flank and rear.

On discovering this movement Lee hastened to strike. A force was sent to assail the retreating column in the rear; but the bridgeless Chickahominy, guarded by artillery, held the pursuers at bay. Lee threw other portions of his army against McClellan's right, at Savage's Station on the 29th, at Frazier's Farm on the day following; but the Union troops each time stood their ground till ready and then continued their march.

July 1st found the retreating host concentrated on Malvern Hill, a plateau a mile and a half long and half as broad, with ravines toward the advancing enemy. Here McClellan planted seventy cannon, rising tier upon tier up the slope, seven heavy siege guns crowning the crest. The po-

sition was impregnable, but Lee determined to attack.   Shortly before sunset his
men advanced boldly to the charge, but
were mowed down by the terrible concen-

General J. E. B. Stuart's Raid
upon Pope's Headquarters,
August 22, 1862, when
Pope's despatch book fell
into the hands of the Confederates.

trated fire of the batteries.   The hill
swarmed with infantry as well, sheltered by
fences and ravines, while shells from the
gunboats in James River could reach every

part of the Confederate line. Yet not till nine in the evening did Lee let the useless carnage cease. Badly demoralized as the opposing army was, McClellan at midnight withdrew to Harrison's Landing, farther down the James.

During the Seven Days' Retreat he had lost 15,000 men; the Confederates somewhat more. Military authorities unite in pronouncing McClellan's change of base "brilliantly executed;" but the campaign as a whole was a failure, discouraging the country as much as Bull Run had done. McClellan prepared and fully expected to move on Richmond again from this new base, but early in August received orders to withdraw from the Peninsula. By the middle of the month the dejected Army of the Potomac was on its way north.

The last of June the Union forces in West Virginia, the Shenandoah Valley, and in front of Washington were consolidated into one army, and the same General Pope who had recently won laurels by the conquest of Island Number Ten, put

in command.   His headquarters, he announced, were to be in the saddle, and
those who had criticised McClellan gave
out that the Union army's days of retreating were past.   McClellan was called from
the Peninsula to strengthen this new movement.

Lee started north to crush Pope before
McClellan should reach him.   Pope had
but 50,000 men against Lee's 80,000, and
fell back across the Rappahannock.   Lee
sent Jackson on a far detour, via Thorough-
fare Gap, to get into his rear and cut his
communications.   Jackson moved rapidly
around to Manassas—one of the most brilliant exploits in all the war—and destroyed
Pope's immense supply depot there.   On
August 29th he was attacked by Pope near
the old battle-field of Bull Run.   The first
day's fight was indecisive, but Confederate
re-enforcements under Longstreet arrived
in time to join in the battle of the next.
McClellan was in no hurry to re-enforce his
rival, but proposed " to leave Pope to get
out of his scrape as he might."   Toward

sunset in the battle of the 30th, Longstreet's column, doubling way around Jackson's right and Pope's left, made a grand
charge, taking Pope straight in the flank.

General Thomas J. ("Stonewall") Jackson.

Porter's corps—the Fifth—part of McClellan's army, stood in the "bloody angle" of
cross-fire. His loss was dreadful—2,000
out of 9,000. Pope was compelled to
retire to Centreville. An engagement at
Chantilly, September 1st, forced a further

retreat to Washington.   Pope resigned, and
his army was merged in the Army of the
Potomac, McClellan commanding all.

Lee now invaded Maryland with 60,000
men.   Already the alarmed North heard him
knocking at its gates.   Hastily re-organiz-
ing the army, McClellan gave chase.   Leaving a force to hold Turner's Gap in South
Mountain, Lee pushed on toward Pennsylvania.   By the battle of South Mountain,
September 14th, Hooker got possession of
the gap, and the Union army poured
through.   Seeing that he must fight, Lee
took up a position on Antietam Creek, a
few miles north of Harper's Ferry.   Jackson had just received the surrender of the
latter place, with 11,000 prisoners, and now
hurried to join Lee.

By the night of September 16th, the
two armies were in battle array on either
side of the creek.   To the rear of the Confederate left lay a cultivated area encircled
by woods, a cornfield in its centre.   At
dawn on the 17th, Hooker opened the battle by a furious charge against the Con-

federate left, and tumbled the enemy out of the woods, across the cornfield, and into the thickets beyond, where he was fronted by Confederate reserves. The carnage was terrific. Re-enforcements under Mansfield

General Edwin V. Sumner.

were sent to Hooker, but driven back across the cornfield. Mansfield was killed and Hooker borne from the field wounded, Sumner coming up barely in time to prevent a rout. Once more the Confederates were pushed through the cornfield into the woods. Here, crouching behind natural

breastworks—limestone ridges waist-high—
the southern ranks delivered so hot a fire
as to repulse Sumner's men.   Thus, all the
morning and into the afternoon the tide
of battle surged back and forth through

General Winfield S. Hancock.

the bloody cornfield, strewn with wounded
and dead.

On the Confederate right no action took
place till late in the day.   Burnside then
attacked and gained some slight advantage.
But re-enforcements from Harper's Ferry
came up and were put in against him,

forcing him back to the creek. During the next day McClellan feared to risk a battle. Being re-enforced, he intended to attack on the following morning; but Lee, who should have been crushed, having but 40,000 men to McClellan's 87,000, slipped away in the night and got safely across the Potomac. The Union loss was 12,400; that of the Confederates probably about the same.

The general dissatisfaction with McClellan's slowness caused his removal early in November, Burnside succeeding him. The new commander, who, as the head of the army, was an amiable failure, proposed to move directly against Richmond, but Lee flung himself in his path at Fredericksburg.

Fredericksburg lies on the south bank of the Rappahannock. Behind the city is a gradually ascending plain, bounded by heights which bend toward the river. Lee's army, 80,000 strong, lay in a semicircle along these heights, its wings touching the river above and below the town. Two rows of batteries, planted on the heights,

swept the plain in front and flank. A
sunken road, sheltered by a stone wall,
ran along the base of the declivity. Burnside's army of 125,000 men occupied a
range of hills on the north side of the
river.

General Ambrose E. Burnside.

Lee's position was very strong; but the
country was impatient for action, and Burnside too readily and without any definite
plan gave the order to attack. December
11th and 12th were spent in crossing the
river on pontoon bridges. The ominous

13th came. The first charge was made by
5,000 of Franklin's men against the Confederate right. The attacking column
broke through the lines and reached the
heights; but it was not supported, and
Confederate reserves drove it back.

About noon an attack was made by
Hancock's and French's corps against the
Confederate left. They advanced over the
plain in two lines, one behind the other.
Suddenly the batteries in front, to left, to
right, poured upon them a murderous fire.
Great gaps were mowed in their ranks.
Union batteries, replying from across the
river, added horror to the din, but helped
little. Still the lines swept on. They grew
thinner and thinner, halted, broke, and
fled.

Again they advanced, this time almost up
to the stone wall. Behind it, hidden from
sight, lay gray ranks four deep. Suddenly
that silent wall burst into flame, and the
advancing lines crumbled away more rapidly than before. Three times more the
gallant fellows came on, bayonets fixed, to

useless slaughter. That deadly wall could not be passed.

The two wings having failed, the Union centre, under Fighting Joe Hooker, was

The Stone Wall at Fredericksburg.

ordered to try. He kept his batteries playing till sunset, hoping to make a breach. Four thousand men were then ordered into the jaws of death. Stripping off knapsacks and overcoats, and relying on the bayonet alone, they charged on the double-quick and with a cheer. They got within twenty yards of the stone wall. Again that sheet of flame! In fifteen minutes it was all over, and they returned as rapidly as they advanced, leaving nearly half their number dead and dying behind. During the day Burnside had had 113,000 men either across the river or ready to cross. Lee's force was 78,000.

Night put an end to the luckless carnage. Burnside's generals dissuaded him from renewing the attack next day, and the army re-crossed the river. They had lost 12,300 men; the Confederates 5,000. A writer to the London *Times* from Lee's headquarters called this December 13th a day "memorable to the historian of the Decline and Fall of the American Republic."

Burnside resigned in January, and Hooker took the command, but he did not assume the offensive till the last of April. Then, leaving three corps under Sedgwick to deceive Lee by a demonstra-

tion in front, he marched up-stream with
the other four of his corps, crossed the
Rappahannock and the Rapidan, partially
turned Lee's left, and took up a position
near Chancellorsville.   It was a perfect

General Oliver O. Howard.

plan, and thus far triumphantly executed.
But here Hooker waited, and the pause
was fatal.   On the night of April 30th
Lee perceived that Sedgwick's movement
was only a feint, and gathered all his
forces, 62,000 strong, to fight at Chancellorsville. He fortified himself so firmly

that Hooker with 64,000, or, including
Sedgwick's two corps and the cavalry,
113,000, made not a single step of further advance.

Nor was this the worst.   Hooker's right

General John Sedgwick.

wing, under Howard, was weakly posted.
On the 2d of May Stonewall Jackson,
who cherished the theory that one man
in an enemy's rear is worth ten in his
front, making a detour of fifteen miles,

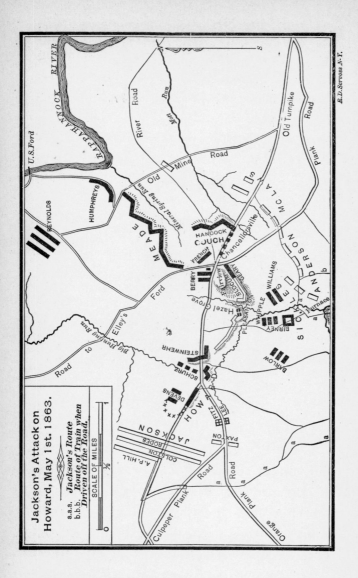

Jackson's Attack on
Howard, May 1st, 1863.

a.a.a. *Jackson's Route*
b.b.b. *Route of Train when
Driven off the Road.*

SCALE OF MILES

0   ½   1

RAPPAHANNOCK RIVER

U.S. Ford

REYNOLDS

HUMPHREYS

MEADE

Old   Mine   Road

River   Road

Mott   Run

River   Road

Mineral Spring Run

Old

Ford

Eley's

Road   to

Big Hunting Run

STEINWEHR

SCHURZ

DEVENS

HOWARD

FITZ LEE

PAXTON

JACKSON

COLSTON

RODES

A. P. HILL

Plank   Road

Culpeper   Plank   Road

Orange   Plank   Road

HANCOCK

COUCH

FRENCH

BERRY

Chancellorsville

SICKLES

Fairview

GEARY

Hazel   Grove

PLEASANTON

WHIPPLE

WILLIAMS

BIRNEY

Furnace

BARLOW

ANDERSON

McLAW

Old Turnpike

Plank   Road

Old Pike

Road

S

S

S

S

a

b

a

a

a

a

a

R. D. Servoss N. Y.

got upon Howard's right unobserved, and
rolled it up. The surprise was as complete as it was inexcusable. Arms were
stacked and the men getting supper. Suddenly some startled deer came bounding
into camp, gray-coats swarming from the
woods hard behind. Almost at the first
charge the whole corps broke and fled.
But the victory cost the Confederates
dear; Jackson was fatally wounded, probably by his own men.

All the next day the Union army fought
on the defensive. Hooker was stunned in
the course of it by a cannon-ball stroke
upon the house-pillar against which he
was leaning, and the army was left without
a commanding mind. Sedgwick, who was
to come up from below Fredericksburg and
take Lee in the rear, found it impossible to
do this in time, having to fight his way
forward with great loss. When he drew
near, Lee was enough at leisure to attend
to him. Forty thousand troops, aching for
the fray, were left idle while Lee was
hammering away against the portion of

the Union line commanded by Sickles.
Ammunition gave out, and charge after
charge had to be repulsed with the bayonet.

Sickles's brave men at last yielded. The
Confederate attack of May 4th was nearly
all directed against Sedgwick, whose noble
corps narrowly escaped capture. That
night the whole army fell back to nearly
its old position north of the Rappahannock.
Except that at Fredericksburg it was the
most disgraceful fiasco on either side during
the war. It cost 17,000 men, and accomplished less than nothing. The South was
elated. It proposed again to invade the
North and this time dictate terms of peace.

Early in June Lee's jubilant army,
strengthened to 100,000, with 15,000 cavalry and 280 guns, started on its second
grand Northern Campaign. It marched
down the Shenandoah Valley, crossed the
Potomac on the 25th, and headed for
Chambersburg, Penn. The Army of the
Potomac marched parallel with it, on the
east side of the Blue Ridge, and crossed

the Potomac a day later. Hooker suddenly resigned, and Meade was put in
command.

Lee reached Chambersburg ; his advance

General James Longstreet.

even pushed well on toward Harrisburg,
the capital of Pennsylvania. At Chambersburg he waited eagerly for those riots
in northern cities by which the "copperheads" had expected to aid his march. In
vain. Meade was drawing near. "Pressed

by the finger of destiny, the Confederate
army went down to Gettysburg," and here
the advance of both hosts met on July 1st.
After some sharp fighting the Union van
was driven back in confusion through
Gettysburg, with a loss of 10,000 men,
half of them prisoners. The brave General Reynolds, commanding the First
Corps, lost his life in this action. The
residue fell back to Cemetery Hill, south
of the town. Meade, fifteen miles to the
south, sent Hancock on to take command
of the field, and see what it was best to
do. This able and trusty officer hurried
to the scene of action in an ambulance,
studying maps as he went. He saw at a
glance the strength of Cemetery Ridge
and resolved to retreat no farther. The
remaining corps were ordered up, and by
noon of July 2d had mostly taken their
positions.

The Union army lay along an elevation
some three miles in length, resembling a
fish-hook in shape. At the extreme southern end, forming the head of the shank,

rose "Round Top," four hundred feet in height. Farther north was "Little Round Top," about three-fourths as high. Cemetery Ridge formed the rest of the shank. The hook curved to the east, with Culp's

General George G. Meade.

Hill for the barb. The Confederate army occupied Seminary Ridge a mile to the west, its left wing, however, bending around to the east through Gettysburg, the line being nearly parallel with Meade's, but much longer. Each army numbered not far from 80,000.

The battle of the second day began about three in the afternoon. Meade had neglected to occupy Little Round Top, which was the key to the Union line. Longstreet's men began climbing its rugged sides. Fortunately the movement was seen in time, and Union troops, after a most desperate conflict, seized and held the crest of the hill.

Along the Union left centre General Sickles's corps had taken a position in advance of the rest of the line, upon a ridge branching off from Cemetery Ridge at an acute angle. Here he was fiercely attacked and most of his force finally driven back into the line of Cemetery Ridge. The Union right had been greatly weakened to strengthen the centre. The Confederates charged here also, and carried the outer intrenchments at Culp's Hill. The Union losses during the afternoon were 10,000— three-fifths in Sickles's corps, which lost half its numbers.

The next morning was spent by Lee in preparing for a grand charge upon the Union centre, that of yesterday upon the left having failed, and the Confederates having this morning been driven from the ground gained the night before on the right at Culp's Hill.   The storm burst about one o'clock.   For two hours 120 guns on Seminary Ridge kept up a furious cannonade, to which Meade replied with 80.   About three the Union cannon ceased firing.   Lee mistakenly thought them silenced, and gave the word to charge.

An attacking column 18,000 strong, made up of fresh troops, the flower of Lee's men, and commanded by the impetuous Pickett, the Ney of the southern army, emerges from the woods on Seminary Ridge, and, drawn up in three lines, one behind the other, with a front of more than a mile, moves silently down the slope and across the valley toward the selected spot. Suddenly the Union batteries again open along the whole line. Great furrows are ploughed in the advancing ranks.   They press steadily on, and

climb the slope toward Meade's lines.
Two regiments behind rude intrenchments
slightly in advance pour in such a murderous fire that the column swerves a little
toward its left, exposing its flank.   General

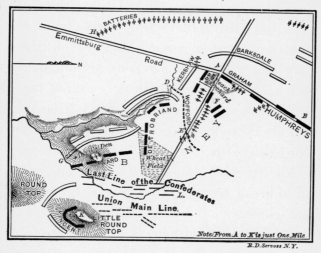

Diagram of the Attack on Sickles and Sykes.

Stannard and his lusty Vermonters make an
irresistible charge upon this.   Windrows of
Pickett's poor fellows are mowed down by
the combined artillery and musketry fire.
A part of the column breaks and flees.   A
part rushes on with desperate valor and

reaches the low stone wall which serves for a Union breastwork. A venomous hand-to-hand fight ensues. Union re-enforcements swarm to the endangered point. The three Confederate brigade commanders are all killed or fatally wounded, whole regiments of their followers surrounded and taken prisoners. The rest are tumbled back, and the broken remnants of that noble column flee in wild confusion across the valley.

The Confederate loss on this eventful day was 16,000, the Union loss not one-fifth as great. General Hancock, whose command bore the brunt of the charge, was severely wounded. Meade should have pressed his advantage, but did not, and next day Lee retreated under cover of a storm and escaped across the Potomac. His losses during the three days had been frightful, amounting to 23,000. In one brigade, numbering 2,800 on July 1st, only 835 answered roll-call three days later. Meade's total losses were also 23,000. Meade had had on the field in all 83,000 men and 300 guns, Lee 69,000 and 250 guns.

Gettysburg marks the turning of the tide. The South's dream of getting a foothold in the North was forever past. She was soon to hear a gallant Northerner's voice demanding the surrender of Richmond.

CHAPTER VIII.

COLLAPSE OF THE CONFEDERACY

GETTYSBURG was the last general engagement in the East during 1863. The next
spring, as we have noticed, Grant was
appointed Lieutenant-General, with command of all the northern armies, now
numbering over 600,000 effectives. This
vast body of men he proposed to use
against the fast-weakening Confederacy in
concerted movements. Sherman's part in
the great plan has already been traced.
The hardest task, that of facing Lee, the
hero of Vicksburg and Chattanooga reserved for himself. Greek thus met
Greek, and the death-grapple began.

May 4th the Army of the Potomac
crossed the Rapidan and entered the
Wilderness, Meade in immediate command, with 120,000 men present for duty.

Lee, heading an army of 62,000 veterans, engaged his new antagonist without delay. For two days the battle raged in the gloomy woods. There was no opportunity for brilliant manœuvres. The men of the two armies lay doggedly behind the trees, each blazing away through the underbrush at an unseen foe, often but a few yards off, while a stream of mangled forms borne on stretchers came steadily pouring to the rear. The tide of battle surged this way and that, with no decisive advantage for either side.

But Grant, as Lee said of him, "was not a retreating man." If he had not beaten, neither had he been beaten. Advance was the word. On the night of the 7th he began that series of "movements by the left flank" which was to force Lee forever from the Rappahannock front. The army stretched nearly north and south, facing west. Warren's corps, at the extreme right, quietly withdrew from the enemy's front, and marching south took a position beyond Hancock's, hitherto the left. Sedg-

wick's corps followed. By this sidling
movement the army worked its way south,
all the while presenting an unbroken front
to the enemy. Yet, on reaching Spottsylvania, Grant found Lee's army there before

Death of General Sedgwick at Spottsylvania, May 9, 1864.

him.   Sharp fighting began again on the
9th and continued three days, but was indecisive, mainly from the wild nature of the
country, heavily timbered, with only occasional clearings.

An early morning attack on the 12th
carried a salient angle in the centre of the
Confederate line, securing 4,000 prisoners
and twenty guns.   All that day and far into
the night Lee desperately strove to dislodge the assailants from this "bloody
angle."   Five furious charges were stubbornly repulsed, the belligerents between
these grimly facing each other from lines
of rifle-pits often but a few feet apart.
Bullets flew thick as hail, a tree eighteen
inches through being cut clean off by
them.   Great heaps of dead and wounded lay between the lines, and "at times
a lifted arm or a quivering limb told of
an agony not quenched by the Lethe
of death around."   Lee did not give up
this death-grapple till three o'clock in
the morning, when he fell back to a new
position.   His losses here in killed and

wounded were about 5,000; Grant's about 6,000.

Rains now compelled both armies to remain quiet for several days. Meantime news reached Grant that Butler, who was to have moved up the James with his army of 20,000 and co-operate with the main army against Richmond, had suffered himself to be "bottled up" at Bermuda Hundred, a narrow spit of land between the James and Appomattox Rivers, the Confederates having "driven in the cork." Re-enforcements reached Grant, however, which made good all his losses.

On the 19th, after an unsuccessful assault the day before, he resumed the flanking movement, and reached and passed the North Anna. But Lee pushed in like a wedge between the two parts of the Union army, separated by crossing the river at different points, and after some fighting, Grant re-crossed and resumed his march to the south. Lee, again moving on shorter lines, reached Cold Harbor before Grant.

The outer line of Confederate intrench-

ments at Cold Harbor was carried on June
1st, and at early dawn on the 3d a charge
made along the whole front.   Under cover
of a heavy artillery fire the men advanced
to the enemy's rifle-pits and carried them.
They then swept on toward the main line.
The ground was open, and the advancing
columns were exposed to a terrible storm
of iron and lead.   Artillery cross-fire swept
through their ranks from right to left.
The troops pressed close up to the works,
but could not carry them. They intrenched, however, and held the position
gained, at some points within thirty yards
of the hostile ramparts.   The Union loss
was very heavy, not less than 6,000; the
Confederates, fighting under shelter, lost
comparatively few.

During the next ten days the men lay
quietly in their trenches.   Both forces had
now moved so far south that Grant's hope
of getting between Lee's army and Richmond had to be abandoned.   He therefore
decided to cross the James and take a position south of Richmond, whence he could

threaten its lines of communication, while that river would furnish him a secure base of supplies.

The two hosts now began a race for Petersburg, an important railway centre, twenty-two miles south of Richmond. Grant's advance reached the town first, but delayed earnest attack, and on the morning of the 15th Lee's veterans, after an all-night's march, flung themselves into the intrenchments. Grant spent the next four days in vain efforts to dislodge them. On the 19th he gave up this method of assault, and began a regular siege. His losses in killed and wounded hereabouts had been almost 9,000.

Things now remained comparatively quiet till late in July. Both sides were busy strengthening their intrenchments. Lee held both Richmond and Petersburg in force, besides a continuous line between the two. Attempts to break this line and to cut the railroads around Petersburg led to several engagements which would have been considered great battles earlier in the war.

Grant's total losses from the crossing of
the Rapidan to the end of June were
61,000, but re-enforcements promptly filled
his ranks. The Confederate loss cannot be

General David Hunter.

accurately determined, but was probably
about two-thirds as great.

Through July one of Burnside's regiments, composed of Pennsylvanians used
to such business, had been working at a
mine under one of the main redoubts in

front of Petersburg. A shaft 500 feet long was dug, with a cross gallery 80 feet in length at the end square under the redoubt. This chamber was charged with 8,000 pounds of powder, which was fired July 30th. The battery and brigade immediately overhead were blown into the air, and the Confederate soldiers far to left and right stunned and stupefied with terror. For half an hour the way into Petersburg was open. Why did none enter? The answer is sad.

Grant had splendidly fulfilled his part by a feint to Deep Bottom across the James, which had drawn thither all but about one division of Lee's Petersburg force. But Meade, at a late hour on the 29th, changed the entire plan of assault, which Burnside had carefully arranged, and to lead which a fresh division had been specially drilled. Then there was lamentable inefficiency or cowardice on the part of several subordinate officers. The troops charged into the great, cellar-like crater, twenty-five feet deep, where, for lack of

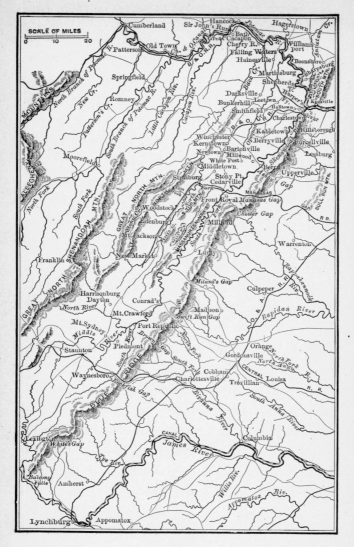

The Shenandoah Valley.

orders, they remained huddled together instead of pushing on. The Confederates rallied, and after shelling the crater till more of its occupants were dead than alive, charged and either routed the living or took them prisoners.

During the summer and fall of 1864 the scene of active operations was shifted to the Shenandoah Valley. The latter part of June Lee sent Early, 20,000 strong, to make a demonstration against Washington, hoping to scare Grant away from Petersburg. Early moved rapidly down the valley, hustling Hunter before him, who escaped only by making a detour to the west, thus leaving Washington open. Thither Early pushed with all speed.

General Lew Wallace hastily gathered up the few troops at his disposal and hurried out from Baltimore to meet him. Wallace was defeated at the Monocacy River July 9th, but precious time was gained for the strengthening of Washington. When Early arrived before the city on the 11th, Grant's re-enforcements had

not yet come, and the fate of the capital
trembled in the balance. Early happily
delayed his attack till the morrow, and
that night two of Grant's veteran corps

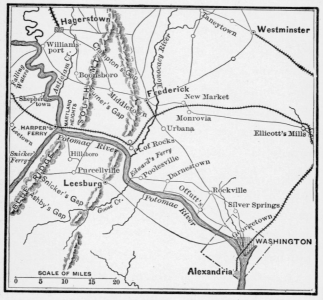

General Early's Maryland Campaign.

landed in Washington, President Lincoln,
in his anxiety, being on the wharf to meet
them. Once more Washington was safe,
and Early fell back, pressed by the new-
comers

The pursuit was feeble, however, and the last of July Early swooped down the valley again. A detachment pushed into Pennsylvania and burned Chambersburg. All through the war the Confederate operations in the Shenandoah Valley had been an annoyance and a menace. Grant now determined to put a definite stop to this, and sent the dashing General Sheridan for the work with 30,000 troops, including 8,000 cavalry. Sheridan pushed Early up the Shenandoah, defeating him at Opequon Creek, September 19th, and at Fisher's Hill two days later.

One-half of Early's army had been destroyed or captured, and the rest driven southward. Sheridan then, in accordance with Grant's orders, that the enemy might no longer make it a base of operations against the capital, laid waste the valley so thoroughly that, as the saying went, not a crow could fly up or down it without carrying rations. Spite of this, Early, having been re-enforced, entered the valley once more. The Union army lay at Cedar

Creek. Sheridan had gone to Washington on business, leaving General Wright in command. On the night of October 18th, the wily Confederate crept around to the rear of the Union left, and attacked at daybreak. Wright was completely surprised, and his left wing fled precipitately, losing 1,000 prisoners and 18 guns. He ordered a retreat to Winchester. The right fell slowly back in good order, interposing a steady front between Early and the demoralized left.

Meanwhile Sheridan, who had reached Winchester on his return, snuffed battle, and hurried to the scene. Now came "Sheridan's Ride." Astride the coal-black charger immortalized by Buchanan Read's verse, he shot ahead and dashed upon the battle-field shortly before noon, his horse dripping with foam. His presence restored confidence, and the army steadily awaited the expected assault. It came, was repulsed, was reciprocated. Early was halted, then pushed, then totally routed, and his army nearly destroyed. It was one of the most signal and telling victories of the war. In a month's campaign Sheridan had killed and wounded 10,000 of the enemy and taken 13,000 prisoners.

All this time the siege of Petersburg was sturdily pressed. In August, Grant got possession of the Weldon Railroad, an important line running south from Petersburg. During the next month fortifications on the Richmond side of the James were carried and held. Through the winter Grant contented himself with gradually extending his lines around Petersburg, trying to cut Lee's communications, and preventing his sending troops against Sherman. He had a death-grip upon the Confederacy's throat, and waited with confidence for the contortions which should announce its death.

The spring of 1865 found the South reduced to the last extremity. The blockade had shut out imports, and it is doubtful if ever before so large and populous a region was so far from being self-sustaining. Even of food-products, save corn and bacon, the dearth became desperate. Wheat bread and salt were luxuries almost from the first. Home-made shoes, with wooden soles and uppers cut from buggy tops or old pocket-books, became the fashion. Pins were eagerly picked up in the streets. Thorns, with wax heads, served as hairpins. Scraps of old metal became precious as gold.

The plight of the army was equally distressing. Drastic drafting had long since taken into the army all the able-bodied men between the ages of eighteen and forty-five. Boys from fourteen to eighteen, and old men from forty-five to sixty, were also pressed into service as junior and senior reserves, the Confederacy thus, as General Butler wittily said, "robbing both the cradle and the grave." Lee's army had been crumbling away beneath the terrible blows dealt it by Grant. He received some re-enforcements during 1864, but in no wise enough to make good his losses. When he took the field in the spring of 1865, his total effective force was 57,000. Grant's army, including Butler's and Sheridan's troops, numbered 125,000.

Lee now perceived that his only hope lay in escaping from the clutches of Grant and making a junction with Johnston's army in North Carolina. Grant was on the watch for precisely this. On March 29th Sheridan worked around into the rear of the Confederate right. Lee descried the movement, and extended his lines that way to obviate it. A force was sent, which drove Sheridan back in some confusion. Re-enforced, he again advanced and beat the forces opposed to him rearward to Five Forks. Here, April 1st, he made a successful charge, before which the foe broke and ran, leaving 4,500 prisoners.

Fearing an attack on Sheridan in force which might let Lee out, Grant sent re-enforcements, at the same time keeping up a roaring cannonade along the whole line all night. At five on the morning of the 2d, a grand assault was made against the Confederate left, which had been weakened to extend the right. The outer intrenchments, with two forts farther in, were taken. Lee at once telegraphed to President Davis

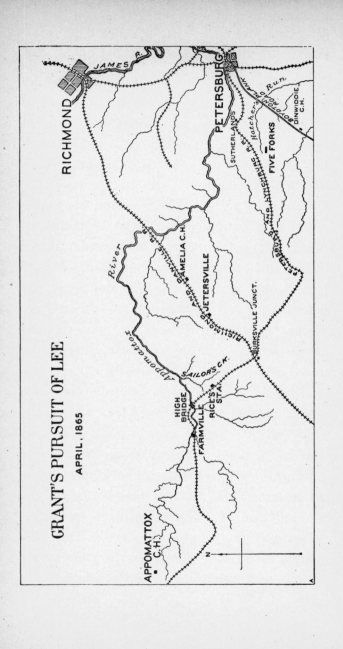

GRANT'S PURSUIT OF LEE

APRIL. 1865

RICHMOND

JAMES R.

PETERSBURG

SUTHERLANDS

FIVE FORKS

Hatchers R.

BOYDTON PLANK RO.

Arthurs Run

DINWIDDIE C.H.

RICHMOND AND DANVILLE R.R.

PETERSBURG AND LYNCHBURG R.R.

AMELIA C.H.

JETERSVILLE

BURKSVILLE JUNCT.

River

Appomattox

SAILOR'S CK.

HIGH BRIDGE

RICE'S STA.

FARMVILLE

APPOMATTOX C.H.

N

that Petersburg and Richmond must be immediately abandoned.

It was Sunday, and the message reached Mr. Davis in church. He hastened out with pallid lips and unsteady tread. A panic-stricken throng was soon streaming from the doomed city. Vehicles let for one hundred dollars an hour in gold. The state-prison guards fled and the criminals escaped. A drunken mob surged through the streets, smashing windows and plundering shops. General Ewell blew up the iron-clads in the river and burned bridges and storehouses. The fire spread till one-third of Richmond was in flames. The air was filled with a "hideous mingling of the discordant sounds of human voices —the crying of children, the lamentations of women, the yells of drunken men—with the roar of the tempest of flame, the explosion of magazines, the bursting of shells." Early on the morning of the 3d was heard the cry, "The Yankees are coming!" Soon a column of blue-coated troops poured into the city, headed by a regiment of colored cavalry, and the Stars and Stripes presently floated over the Confederate capital.

The Confederacy was tottering to its fall. Lee had begun his retreat on the night of the 2d, and was straining every nerve to reach a point on the railroad fifty miles to the west, whence he could move south and join Johnston. Grant was too quick for him. Sending Sheridan in advance to head him off, he himself hurried after with the main army. Gray and blue kept up the race for several days, moving on nearly parallel lines. Sheridan struck the Confederate column at Sailor's Creek on the 6th, and a heavy engagement ensued, in which the southern army lost many wagons and several thousand prisoners.

Lee's band was in a pitiable plight. Its supplies had been cut off, and many of the soldiers had nothing to eat except the young shoots of trees. They fell out of the ranks by hundreds, and deserted to their homes near by. With all hope of escape cut off, and his army dropping to pieces around him, Lee was at last forced to surrender. To this end he met Grant, on April 9th, at a residence near Appomattox Court House.

The personal appearance of the two generals at this interview presented a striking, not to say ludicrous, contrast. Lee, who was a tall, handsome man, was attired in a new uniform, showing all the insignia of his rank, with a splendid dress-sword at his side. Grant, wholly unprepared for the interview, wore a private's uniform, covered with mud and dust from hard riding that day. His shoulder-straps were the only mark of his high rank, and he had no sword. Having served together in the Mexican War, they spent some time in a friendly conversation about those old scenes. Grant then wrote out the terms of surrender, which Lee accepted. The troops were to give their paroles not to take up arms again until properly exchanged, and officers might retain their side-arms, private horses, and baggage. Anxious to heal the wounds of the South,

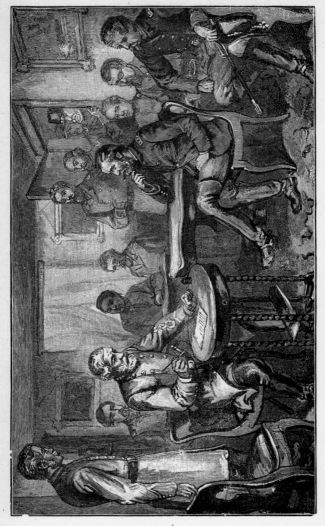

General Lee Signing the Terms of Surrender at Appomattox Court-House

Grant, with rare thoughtfulness, allowed privates also to take home their own horses. "They will need them for the spring ploughing," he said. The 19,000 prisoners captured during the last ten days, together with deserters, left, in Lee's once magnificent army, but 28,356 soldiers to be paroled. The surrendering general was compelled to ask 25,000 rations for these famished troops, a request which was cheerfully granted.

While all loyal hearts were rejoicing over the news of Lee's surrender, recognized as virtually ending the war, a pall suddenly fell upon the land. On the evening of April 14th, while President Lincoln was sitting in a box at Ford's Theatre in Washington, an actor, John Wilkes Booth, crept up behind him, placed a pistol to his head, and fired. Brandishing his weapon, and crying, "*Sic semper tyrannis*," the assassin leaped to the stage, sustaining a severe injury. Regaining his feet, he shouted, "The South is avenged!" and made his escape.

The bullet had pierced the President's

brain and rendered him insensible. He was removed to a house near by, where he died next morning. His body was taken to Springfield, Ill., for burial, and a nation mourned above his grave, as no American since Washington had ever been mourned for before. The South repudiated and deplored the foul deed. Well it might, for, had Lincoln lived, much of its sorrow during the next years would have been avoided.

Booth was only one of a band of conspirators who had intended also to take off General Grant and the whole Cabinet. By a strange good fortune Secretary Seward, sick in bed, was the only victim besides the President. He was stabbed three times with a bowie-knife, but not fatally. After a cunning flight and brave defence Booth was captured near Port Royal, and killed. Of the other conspirators some were hanged, some imprisoned.

The Confederacy collapsed. Johnston's army surrendered to Sherman on April 26th. President Davis fled south. On May 10th he was captured in Georgia, muffled in a lady's cloak and shawl, and became a prisoner at Fortress Monroe. The war had called into military (land) service in the two armies together hardly fewer than 4,000,000 men ; 2,750,000, in round numbers, on the Union side, and 1,250,000 on the other. The largest number of northern soldiers in actual service at any one time was 1,000,516, on May 1, 1865, 650,000 of them being able for duty. The largest number of Confederate land forces in service at any time was 690,000, on January 1, 1863. The Union armies lost by death 304,369—44,238 of these being killed in battle, 49,205 dying of wounds. Over 26,000 are known to have died in Confederate prisons.

CHAPTER IX.

THE WAR ON THE SEA

NAVAL operations during the war fall into three great classes : Those upon inland waters, the Mississippi especially ; those along the coast ; and those upon the high seas. The first class has already been touched upon in connection with the Mississippi campaigns. The naval work along the coast and upon the high seas is, the subject of the present chapter. Only the more important features can be sketched. At the outbreak of the Rebellion our navy was totally unprepared for war. Forty-two vessels were in commission, but most of them were in distant seas or in southern ports. The service was weak with secession sentiment. Between March and July, 1861, 259 naval officers resigned or were dismissed.

Secretary Welles went energetically to work. Vessels in foreign waters were called home, the keels of new craft laid in northern dockyards, and stout merchant

Gideon Welles.

ships bought and fitted up for the rough usage of war. By the end of 1861 the navy numbered 264 vessels. At the close of the war it had 671 ships, carrying 4,610 guns and 50,000 sailors.

The first work—a gigantic one—was to

blockade the southern ports. This involved the constant patrolling of more than 3,000 miles of dangerous coast, indented with innumerable inlets, sounds, and bays. But within a year a fairly effective blockade was in force from Virginia to Texas, drawn tighter and tighter as the navy increased in size. The effectiveness of the blockade is sufficiently proved by the dearth at the South. The South had cotton enough to sell—$300,-000,000 worth in gold at the end of the war—and Europe was greedy to buy; but she could not get her wares to market. Fifteen hundred prizes, worth $30,000,-000, were taken during the war.

The details of the blockade must be left to the reader's imagination. Important as the work was, it was comparatively monotonous and dull—ceaseless watching day and night in all weather, week after week and month after month. Now and then the routine would be broken by the excitement of a chase. A suspicious-looking sail would be spied in the offing and pursued, perhaps, far out to sea. Again, the low hull of a blockade-runner would be seen creeping around a point and heading for the open sea. Or on a still night the throb of engines and the splash of paddle-wheels would give warning that some guilty vessel was trying to steal into port under cover of darkness. Then came the flare of rockets to notify the rest of the blockading fleet, the hot pursuit with boilers crowded to bursting, the boom of the big guns fired at random in the dark, and the exultation of a capture or the disappointment of failure.

Blockade-running became a regular business, enormously profitable. Moonless and cloudy nights were of course the most favorable times for eluding the blockade; but the swift steamers, sitting low in the water and painted a light neutral tint, could not easily be detected by day at a little distance, especially as they burned smokeless coal. The bolder skippers would take all chances. Under cover of a fog they would steal into or out of harbor at risk of going aground, or set sail boldly on a bright moonlight night, when the blockaders would naturally relax their vigilance a little. Occasionally some dare-devil would crowd on all steam and dash openly through the sentinel fleet, trusting to speed to escape being hit or captured. When hard pressed, the blockade-runner would beach his craft, set it afire, and take to the woods. At the close of the war thirty wrecks of blockade-runners were rotting on the sands near Charleston Harbor.

In connection with the blockade a number of naval expeditions were sent against various points along the coast. In October, 1861, a fleet under Flag-Officer Dupont, consisting of a steam frigate, a dozen or more gunboats, with numerous transports and coaling-schooners, and carrying 12,000 troops under General T. W. Sherman, set sail from Hampton Roads for Port Royal, S. C. After a stormy passage the fleet anchored off the harbor on November 4th. On opposite sides of the entrance, two and a half miles apart, stood Forts

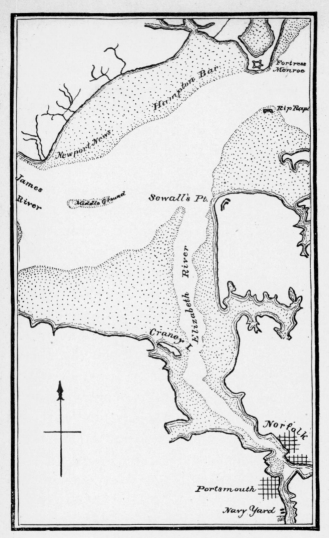

Map of Hampton Roads.

Walker and Beauregard—strong earth-works, mounting one 23 the other 20 guns, and garrisoned by 1,700 men. The 7th dawned bright and clear, the sea smooth as glass. About nine o'clock the bombard-ment began. The fleet steamed slowly round and round in an ellipse between the forts, each vessel as it came within range pouring in its fire, then passing on and waiting its turn to fire again. The can-nonade was concentrated upon Fort Walker. The moving ships offered a poor mark to the fort, while the aim of the fleet was very accurate, covering the gun-ners with sand and dismounting the guns. After four hours' action Fort Walker was evacuated, and soon Fort Beauregard also in consequence.

Port Royal was the finest harbor on the coast, and was of great value to the navy all through the war as a repair and supply station. Dupont sent out expeditions, and by the end of the year had possession of a large part of the coast of South Carolina and Georgia. In the following spring ex-

peditions from Port Royal regained Fer-
nandina and St. Augustine on the Florida
coast. In April Fort Pulaski, a strong
brick work at the mouth of the Savannah
River, was reduced by eleven batteries
planted on a neighboring island, its surrender completing the blockade of Savannah.

Albemarle and Pamlico Sounds, on the
coast of North Carolina, swarmed with
blockade-runners. Rivers, canals, and railroads formed a network of communications
with the interior, and vessels were constantly slipping to sea with cargoes of
cotton, to return with munitions of war.
Hatteras Inlet, seized in August, 1861,
was not a sufficient basis for the blockade.
In February, 1862, a fleet bearing 11,500
soldiers, under General Burnside, arrived
at Roanoke Island, which lies between the
two great sounds. The troops were landed,
and on the 8th, charging over marshy
ground, sometimes waist-deep in water, carried the batteries and gained possession of
the island. Newbern, one of the most
important ports of North Carolina, was

captured a month later, and Fort Macon, commanding the entrance to Beaufort Harbor, surrendered in April.

Meanwhile what had the Confederates been doing in naval matters? When the Norfolk navy-yard was abandoned in April, 1861, the fine old frigate Merrimac was scuttled. She was raised by the Davis Government and converted into an iron-clad ram—a novelty in those days. The hull was cut down to the water's edge, and a stout roof, 170 feet long, with sloping sides and a flat top, built amidships and plated with four inches of iron. This roof was pierced for ten guns—four rifles and six nine-inch smooth-bores.

On March 8, 1862, the Union fleet, consisting of the Cumberland, Congress, Minnesota, and some smaller craft, rode lazily at anchor in Hampton Roads. About noon a curious looking structure was seen coming down Elizabeth River. It was the Merrimac. She steered straight for the Cumberland. The latter poured in a broadside from her heavy ten-inch guns, but the

The Sinking of the Frigate Cumberland by the Merrimac in Hampton Roads, March 8, 1862.

balls glanced off the ram's sloping iron sides like peas. The Merrimac's iron beak crashed into the Cumberland's side, making a great hole. In a few minutes the old war-sloop, working her guns to the water's edge, went down in fifty-four feet of water, 120 sick and wounded sinking with her.

The Congress had meanwhile been run aground. The Merrimac fired hot shot, setting her afire. Nearly half the crew being killed or wounded, she surrendered, her magazine exploding and blowing her up at midnight. The Minnesota, hastening up with two other vessels from Fortress Monroe to aid her sisters, had run aground. Being of heavy draught, the Merrimac could not get near enough to do her much damage, and at nightfall steamed back to her landing. As the telegraph that night flashed over the land the news of the Merrimac's victory, dismay filled the North, exultation the South. What was to stay the career of the invulnerable monster? Could it not destroy the whole United States navy of wooden ships?

Next morning the Merrimac reappeared to complete her work of destruction. As she drew near the stranded Minnesota, a strange little craft moved out from the side of the big frigate and headed straight for the iron-clad. It was Ericsson's Monitor, which had arrived from New York at midnight. The Confederate characterization of it as a "cheese-box on a raft" is still the best description of its appearance. Its lower hull, 122 feet long and 34 wide, was protected by a raft-like overhanging upper hull, 172 feet long and 41 wide. Midway upon her low deck, which rose only a foot above the water, stood a revolving turret 21 feet in diameter and nine in height. It was made of iron eight inches thick, and bore two eleven-inch guns throwing each a 180-pound ball. Near the bow rose the pilot-house, made of iron logs nine inches by twelve in thickness. The side armor of the hull was five inches thick, and the deck was covered with heavy iron plates.

For three hours the iron-clads fought.

John Ericsson.

The Merrimac's shot glanced harmlessly
off the round turret, while her attempts to
run the Monitor down failed.   Meanwhile

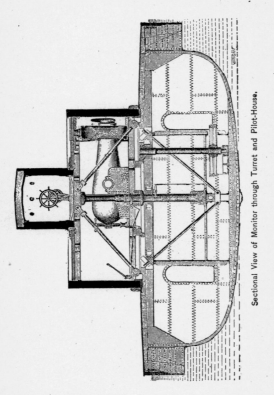

Sectional View of Monitor through Turret and Pilot-House.

the big guns in the Monitor's turret, firing
every seven minutes, were pounding the
ram's sides with terrible blows.   The Merri-

mac's armor was at points crushed in several inches, but nowhere pierced. About noon the fight stopped, as if by mutual consent. It was a drawn battle, but the career of the Merrimac had ended. Upon McClellan's advance, in May, she was blown up. The Monitor received no serious injury in this action, but the next December she foundered in a storm off Cape Hatteras.

The invention of the Monitor revolutionized naval warfare, and set European nations to building the ponderous iron-clad navies of the present day. The United States Government soon contracted for twenty single-turret monitors, and four double-turreted ones with fifteen-inch guns.

The Confederates now went to building iron-clads on the model of the Merrimac. On the morning of January 31, 1863, the iron-clads Palmetto State and Chicora steamed out of Charleston Harbor, in a dense fog, and attacked the blockading fleet of wooden vessels. After ramming one ship and sending a shot through the boiler of another, they put back to port.

In April, Admiral Dupont tried to seize Charleston Harbor with his fleet of seven monitors and two iron-clads. In a two hours' action the monitors were seriously injured by the heavy guns of the forts, and the fleet withdrew. In August, land batteries reduced Fort Sumter almost to ruins, and in the following month Fort Wagner was abandoned. June 17th, the iron-clad Atlanta, armed with a torpedo at the end of a spar, ran down from Savannah to engage with two monitors guarding the mouth of the river. She got aground, rendering the torpedo useless. The fifteen-inch guns of the monitors pierced her armor, and in a few minutes she surrendered.

The Albemarle proved a more dangerous foe. The last of April, 1864, it descended Roanoke River, smashed the gunboats at the mouth, and compelled the surrender of the forts and the town of Plymouth. A few days later it attacked a fleet of gunboats below the mouth of the river. After a severe tussle, inflicting and receiving considerable damage, it steamed back to Plymouth. Here it lay at the wharf till October, when it was sunk by Lieutenant Cushing, already famous for daring exploits under the very noses of the enemy. On the night of October 27th, young Cushing approached the ironclad in a steam launch with a torpedo at the end of a spar projecting from the bow. Jumping his boat over the log boom surrounding the ram, in the thick of musketry fire from deck and shore, Cushing calmly worked the strings by which the intricate torpedo was fired. It exploded under the

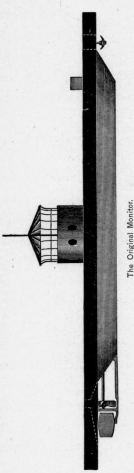

The Original Monitor.

vessel's overhang, and she soon sunk. At the moment of the explosion a cannon-ball crashed through the launch. Cushing plunged into the river and swam to shore through a shower of bullets. After crawling through the swamps next day, he found a skiff and paddled off to the fleet. Of the launch's crew of fourteen, only one other escaped.

The stronghold of the Confederacy on the Gulf was Mobile. Two strong forts, mounting twenty-seven and forty-seven guns, guarded the channel below the city, which was further defended by spiles and torpedoes. In the harbor, August 5, 1864, lay the iron-clad ram, Tennessee, and three gunboats, commanded by Admiral Buchanan, formerly captain of the Merrimac. Farragut determined to force a passage. Before six o'clock in the morning his fleet of four monitors and fourteen wooden ships, the latter lashed together two and two, got under way, Farragut taking his station in the main rigging of the Hartford. The action opened about

seven.   One of the monitors struck a torpedo and sunk.   The Brooklyn, which was
leading, turned back to go around what
seemed to be a nest of torpedoes.   The
whole line was in danger of being huddled
together under the fire of the forts.   Farragut boldly took the lead, and the fleet
followed.   The torpedo cases could be
heard rapping against the ships' bottoms,
but none exploded.

The forts being safely passed, the Confederate gunboats advanced to the attack.
One of these was captured, the other two
escaped.   The powerful iron-clad Tennessee now moved down upon the Union fleet.
It was 209 feet long, with armor from five
to six inches thick.   Farragut ordered his
wooden vessels to run her down.   Three
succeeded in ramming her squarely.   She
reeled under the tremendous blows, and
her gunners could not keep their feet.   A
monitor sent a fifteen-inch ball through
her stern.   Her smoke-stack and steering-
chains were shot away, and several port
shutters jammed.   About ten A.M., after

an action of an hour and a quarter, the
ram hoisted the white flag.   The forts surrendered in a few days.

January 15, 1865, Fort Fisher, a strong
work near Wilmington, N. C., mounting
seventy-five guns, was captured by a joint
land and naval expedition under General
Terry and Admiral Porter.   This was the
last great engagement along the coast.

The story of the war upon the high seas
is quickly told.   Swift and powerful cruisers
were built in English ship-yards, with the
connivance of the British Government,
whence they sailed to prey upon our commerce.   The Florida, Georgia, Shenandoah, Chameleon, and Tallahassee, were
some of the most famous in the list of
Confederate cruisers.   During 1861, fifty-
eight prizes were taken by them.   American merchant vessels were driven from the
sea.   The Shenandoah alone destroyed over
$6,000,000 worth in vessels and cargoes.

The two most celebrated of these sea-
rovers were the Sumter and the Alabama,
both commanded by Captain Semmes, for-

merly of the United States Navy. The
Sumter was a screw steamer of 600 tons, a
good sailer and sea-boat. She was bought
by the Confederate Government and armed
with a few heavy guns. On June 30, 1861,
she ran the blockade at Charleston, and
began scouring the seas. All through the
fall she prowled about the Atlantic, taking seventeen prizes, most of which were
burned. Many United States cruisers were
sent after her, but she eluded or escaped
them all. Early in 1862 the Sumter entered the port of Gibraltar. Here she was
blockaded by two Union gunboats, and
Semmes finally sold her to take command
of the Alabama.

The Alabama was built expressly for the
Confederacy at Laird's ship-yard, Liverpool,
and although her character was perfectly
well known, the British Government permitted her to go to sea. She was taken
to one of the Azores Islands, where she
received her armament and her captain.
The officers were Confederates, the crew
British. She began her destructive career

in August, 1862. By the last of October
she had taken twenty-seven prizes. In
January she sunk the gunboat Hatteras,
one of the blockading fleet off Galveston,
Tex. After cruising in all seas, the Alabama, in 1864, returned to the European
coast, having captured sixty-five vessels
and destroyed property worth between
$6,000,000 and $7,000,000.

On June 11th, Semmes put into the harbor of Cherbourg, on the coast of France.
Captain Winslow, commanding the United
States steamer Kearsarge, cruising in the
neighborhood, heard of the famous rover's
arrival, and took his station outside the
harbor. About ten o'clock on the morning
of June 19, 1864, the Alabama was seen
coming out of port, attended by a French
man-of-war and an English steam yacht.
Captain Winslow immediately cleared the
decks for action. It was a clear, bright
day, with a smooth sea. The fight took
place about seven miles from shore. The
two ships were pretty equally matched,
each being of about 1,000 tons burden.

The Kearsarge had the heavier smooth-bore guns, but the Alabama carried a 100-pound Blakely rifle. The Kearsarge was protected amidships by chain cables.

The Alabama opened the engagement. The Kearsarge replied with a cool and accurate fire. The action soon grew spirited. Solid shot ricochetted over the smooth water. Shells crashed against the sides or exploded on deck. The two ships sailed round and round a common centre, keeping about half a mile apart. In less than an hour the Alabama was terribly shattered and began to sink. She tried to escape, but water put out her engine fires. Semmes hoisted the white flag. In a few minutes the Alabama went down, her bow rising high in the air. Boats from the Kearsarge rescued some of the crew. The English yacht picked up others, Semmes among them, thus running off with Winslow's prisoners. The Kearsarge had received little damage.

The sinking of the Alabama ended the

The Sinking of the Alabama.

career of the Confederate cruisers. American commerce had been nearly driven from
the ocean, and, moreover, the days of
peace on land and sea alike were near at
hand.

CHAPTER X.

FOREIGN RELATIONS—FINANCES—EMANCI-PATION

A CIVIL war of vast proportions in the world's greatest republic naturally aroused deep interest among the monarchies of Europe. Russia evinced warm friendliness to the United States. The rest of the world, save England and France, showed us no ill-will.

England, with unfriendly haste, admitted the belligerent rights of the Confederacy before Mr. Adams, our minister, could reach the British court. The North was surprised and shocked that liberty-loving, conservative England should so far side with "rebellious slave-holders." It would seem that, besides sympathy with the aristocratic structure of southern society, national envy helped to put England into this false position.   Commercial interests had greater weight.   Four millions of people in England depended upon cotton manufactures for support.   Three-fourths of the cotton they had used came from our southern ports, which the blockade closed. Moreover, the Confederacy declared for free trade, while the North adopted a high war tariff which drove many English goods out of American markets.   The London *Times* complained that nearly $4,000,000 worth of English cutlery alone had been made worthless by our tariff.

An incident early in the war heightened the ill-will between the two countries.   On a dark night in October, 1861, Messrs. Mason and Slidell, Confederate commissioners to England and France, ran the blockade at Charleston, and soon after took passage at Havana on the English mail steamer Trent.   November 8th, 250 miles out from Havana, the United States sloop of war San Jacinto, Captain Wilkes, compelled the Trent, by a shot across her bows, to heave to, and took off the commissioners.

All England was hot with resentment. Troops were shipped to Canada, and other war preparations begun. A special messenger was hurried to Washington, demanding an apology and the release of the prisoners. Wilkes's action, though without authority in international law, was warmly approved by the people. The House of Representatives tendered him a vote of thanks. But the Government disavowed the seizure and gave up the commissioners. Mr. Seward, Secretary of State, in a dignified reply to England, insisted that the seizure was fully justified by England's own practice of searching neutral vessels on the high seas; but that, as the United States had always condemned this practice, the prisoners would be released, especially as Captain Wilkes should have brought the Trent before a prize court instead of deciding the validity of the prize himself. The action of the Government, though unpopular at the time, was undoubtedly as prudent as it was just. We could not afford to provoke war with England.

The Landing of the Allied Troops at Vera Cruz.

Our real grievance against Great Britain was that the Queen's proclamation of neutrality was not obeyed. Confederate cruisers were built in English yards, whence they publicly and boastfully sailed to prey upon our then vast merchant marine. Crews as well as ships were English. The British ministry were perfectly aware of their destination, but used all manner of artifices to avoid interfering.

Our most vicious enemy abroad was Napoleon III., so profuse yet so hypocritical in his professions of good-will. He, too, hastened to accord belligerent rights to the Confederacy. Had England not been too wary to join him, the two nations would certainly have recognized the South's independence. Napoleon was on the point of doing this alone. Seven war-vessels were, with his sanction, built for the Confederates at Bordeaux and Nantes, though he was too wily to allow them to sail when he became aware that their destination was fully known to our minister.

Far-reaching political schemes were at

the bottom of Napoleon's wish for a dismembered Union. He was plotting to restore European influence in America by setting up an empire on the ruins of the Mexican republic, and he knew that the United States would never allow this while her power was unbroken. In the latter part of 1861 a French army invaded Mexico. The feeble government was overthrown after a year or two of fighting. In 1863 an empire was established, and Napoleon offered the throne to the Austrian archduke Maximilian. Meanwhile, the protests of the United States were disregarded. But when our hands were freed by the collapse of the Confederacy, Napoleon changed his tone. The French troops were withdrawn early in 1867, and Maximilian was left to his fate. The unhappy prince, betrayed by his own general, fell into the hands of the old Mexican Government, now in the ascendant, and was tried by court-martial and shot. It should be remembered, however, that France's unfriendly attitude all through the Rebellion was maintained by her unscrupulous emperor and did not reflect the wish of the French people.

The expenses of the war were colossal. From beginning to close they averaged $2,000,000 a day, sometimes running up to $3,500,000. The expenditure for the fiscal year ending July 1, 1865, was nearly $2,000,000,000. Of this the War Department required, in round numbers, $1,000,-000,000; the navy department, $123,000,-000. These figures reveal the vast scale upon which the war was waged by land and sea. The national debt rose with frightful rapidity. It was $64,000,000 in 1860, $1,100,000,000 in 1863, $2,800,000,-000 (the highest point reached) in 1865. State and local war debts would swell the amount to more than $4,000,000,000.

The position of Secretary of the Treasury during the war was anything but a bed of roses. The ordinary national income was hardly a drop in the bucket compared with the enormous and constantly increasing expenses. The total receipts for the year ending July 1, 1860, were only $81,000,000. How should the vast sums needed to carry on the war be raised? Resort was had to two sources of revenue—taxation and loans.

A considerable revenue was already derived from customs imposed upon imported goods. In 1861, and again in 1863, tariffs were raised enormously, professedly to increase the revenue. These high rates in a measure defeated their own purpose, altogether stopping the importation of not a few articles.

The war compelled the Government to resort to internal taxation—always unpopular and now unknown in the United States for nearly half a century. Taxes were laid upon almost everything—upon trades, incomes, legacies, manufactures. The words of Sydney Smith will apply to our internal taxes during the war: "Taxes on the ermine which decorates the judge, and the rope which hangs the criminal; on the poor man's salt and the rich man's spice; on the brass nails of

the coffin and the ribands of the bride."
The tax on many finished products ranged
from eight to fifteen per cent. ; on some
it rose to twenty per cent.

But these taxes, severe as they were,

Maximilian Watching the Departure of the Last French Troops from
the City of Mexico.

could furnish only a small part of the necessary income. The Government must borrow. In the first year of the war the banks loaned the United States $150,000,-000 at 7.3 per cent. interest. Many other loans were secured as the war went on— one for $500,000,000, another for $900,000,-000. As security the Government issued bonds, bearing various rates of interest and payable after a certain number of years. Treasury notes were also issued and made legal tender for all debts public and private. As the Government paid its own debts with them, they were in the nature of a forced loan. Of those which bore no interest (commonly known as greenbacks) $433,000,000 were issued from first to last. Also, when property was seized for the use of the army, the owners were given certificates of indebtedness which entitled the holders to payment at the United States Treasury.

The proportion of revenue derived from each of the above sources is illustrated by the report of the treasurer of the United

States for the year ending July 1, 1865. Customs yielded $85,000,000, internal revenue $209,000,000, loans $1,470,000,000.

Finance legislation during the war was more patriotic than wise, due partly to necessary haste, largely to ignorance. The internal taxes bore very unequally upon different classes. The tariff was ill-adjusted to the internal taxes, letting in at low rates some classes of goods whose home production was heavily taxed, thus discriminating in favor of the foreigner. Millions of debt and half the other economic evil of the war might have been saved by doing more to keep the paper dollar on a par with gold. Thus the banks should not have been compelled to pay in gold the loan of 1861. It forced them to suspend specie payment altogether, December 31st of that year— those of New York City first, followed by others everywhere, and by the United States itself. Gold had been at a nominal premium all through 1861, but the first recorded sale at an advance was on January 13, 1862. It would have been better, also, to resort earlier to heavy loans, even at high rates, instead of flooding the country with greenbacks. The national banks, which were created on purpose to help the sale of government bonds, should have been forced to purchase new bonds instead of supplying themselves with bonds already issued, their purchase of which did the Government no good whatever. Neglect in these regards caused the paper dollar to fall in value. In July, 1864, it was worth only thirty-five cents in gold.

The finances of the Confederacy went steadily from bad to worse. The blockade cut off its revenue from import duties. Its poor credit forbade large loans. The government had to rely mainly upon paper money. This soon became almost worthless. In December, 1861, it took $120 in paper money to buy $100 in gold; in 1863 it took $1,900; in 1864, $5,000. Nearly $1,000,000,000 in paper money was issued in all. The Confederate debt at the close of the war was $2,000,000,000. Under the combined influence of depreciated currency

Salmon Portland Chase, Secretary of the Treasury during the Civil War.

and scarcity of goods, prices became ludicrously high.   As early as 1862 flour was $40 a barrel and salt $1 a pound.   Before the war was over, a pound of sugar brought $75, a spool of thread $20.   Toward the end of the war a Confederate soldier, just paid off, went into a store to buy a pair of boots.   The price was $200.   He handed the store-keeper a $500 bill.   "I can't change this."   "Oh, never mind," replied the paper millionnaire.   "I never let a little matter like $300 interfere with a trade." Of course when the Confederacy collapsed all this paper money became absolutely worthless.

Mr. Lincoln and the Republican Party resorted to arms not intending the slightest alteration in the constitutional status of slavery.   But the presence of Union armies on slave soil led to new and puzzling questions.   What should be done with slaves escaping to the Union lines?   Generals Buell and Hooker authorized slave-holders to search their camps for runaway slaves. Halleck gave orders to drive them out of his lines. Butler, alleging that since slaves helped "the rebels" by constructing fortifications they were contraband of war, refused to return those fleeing into his camp. Congress moved up to this position in August, 1861, declaring that slaves used for hostile purposes should be confiscated. But when Fremont and Hunter issued orders freeing slaves in their military districts, President Lincoln felt obliged to countermand them, fearing the effect upon slave States that were still loyal.

As the war went on the conviction grew that peace would never be safe or permanent if slavery remained, and that the suppression of the Rebellion was postponed, jeopardized, and made costlier by every hour of slavery's life. Slaves raised crops, did camp work, and built fortifications, releasing so many more whites for service in hostile ranks, instead of doing all this, and fighting, even, for the Union.

It is interesting to trace the growth of emancipation sentiment during 1862 as it is reflected in congressional legislation. In

March army officers were forbidden to return fugitive slaves.   In April slavery was
abolished in the District of Columbia, with
compensation to owners.   At the same
time Congress adopted a pet scheme of
Mr. Lincoln's, offering compensation to any
State that would free its slaves.   None accepted.   There were about 3,000 slaves in
the District.   Upon the day of their emancipation they assembled in churches and
gave thanks to God.   In June slavery in
the Territories—that bone of contention
through so many years—was forever pro-
hibited.   In July an act was passed freeing
rebels' slaves coming under the Government's protection, and authorizing the use
of negro soldiers.

Already President Lincoln was meditat-
ing universal emancipation.   September
22d the friends of liberty were made glad
by a preliminary proclamation, announcing
the President's intention to free the slaves
on January 1, 1863, should rebellion then
continue to exist.   It is said that Mr. Lincoln would have given this notice earlier

but for the gloomy state of military affairs. The day comes. The proclamation goes forth that all persons held as slaves in the rebellious sections "are and henceforth shall be free." The blot which had so long stained our national banner was wiped away. The Constitution of course does not expressly authorize such an act by the President, but Mr. Lincoln defended it as a "necessary war measure," "warranted by the Constitution upon military necessity."

This bold, epoch-making deed, the death-warrant of slavery here and throughout the world, evoked serious hostility even at the North. The elections in the fall of 1862 and the spring of 1863 showed serious losses for the administration party. Emancipation, too, doubtless added rancor and verve for a time to southern belligerency. But the fresh union, spirit, and strength it soon brought to the northern cause were tenfold compensation. Besides, it vastly exalted our struggle in the moral estimate of Christendom, and lessened danger of foreign intervention.

The War President trod at no time a
path of flowers. Strong and general as
was Union sentiment at the North, ex-
tremely diverse feelings and views prevailed
touching the methods and spirit which
should govern the conduct of the war.
Certain timid, discouraged, or disappointed
Republicans, seeing the appalling loss of
blood and treasure as the war went on, and
the Confederacy's unexpected tenacity of
life, demanded peace on the easiest terms
inclusive of intact Union. Secretaries
Seward and Chase were for a time in this
temper. The doctrinaire abolitionists bitterly assailed President and Congress for
not making, from the outset, the extirpation
of slavery the main aim of hostilities.
Even the great emancipation pacified them
but little.

The Democrats proper entered a far more
sensible, in fact a not wholly groundless,
complaint exactly the contrary. They
charged that the Administration, in hopes
to exhibit the Democracy as a peace party
(which from 1862 it more and more be-

came), *was* making the overthrow of slavery its main aim, waging war for the negro instead of for the Union. They complained also that not only in anti-slavery measures but in other things as well, notably in suspending *habeas corpus*, the Administration was grievously infringing the Constitution.

Yet a fourth class, a democratic rump of southern sympathizers, popularly called "copperheads," wishing peace at any price, did their best to encourage the Rebellion. They denounced the war as cruel, needless, and a failure. They opposed the draft for troops, and were partly responsible for the draft riots in 1863. Many of them were in league with southern leaders, and held membership in treasonable associations. Some were privy to, if not participant in, devilish plots to spread fire and pestilence in northern camps and cities. Partly through influence of the more moderate, several efforts to negotiate peace were made, fortunately every one in vain.

But despite the attacks of enemies and the importunities of weak or short-sighted friends, President Lincoln steadily held on his course. The masses of the people rallied to his support, and in the presidential election of 1864 he was re-elected by an overwhelming majority, receiving 212 electoral votes against 21 for General McClellan, the democratic candidate.

CHAPTER XI.

RECONSTRUCTION

THOUGH arms were grounded, there remained the new task, longer and more perplexing, if not more difficult, than the first, of restoring the South to its normal position in the Union. It was, from the nature of the case, a delicate one. The proud and sensitive South smarted under defeat and was not yet cured of the illusions which had led her to secede. Salve and not salt needed to be rubbed into her wounds. The North stood ready to forgive the past, but insisted, in the name of its desolate homes and slaughtered President, that the South must be restored on such conditions that the past could never be repeated. The difficulty was heightened by the lack of either constitutional provision or historical precedent. Not strange,

in due time ~~will it meet~~ the beneficial changes of the executive will recommend that

all citizens of the United States who shall have remained loyal thereto throughout the rebellion, shall (upon the restoration of the Constitutional relation between the United States, and their respective states, and people, if that relation shall have been suspended or disturbed) be compensated for all losses by acts of the United

Done at the City of Washington, this twenty-second day of September, in the year of our Lord, one thousand, eight hundred and sixty-two, and of the Independence of the United States the eighty-seventh.

Abraham Lincoln

By the President:
William H. Seward,
Secretary of State.

Facsimile of a portion of President Lincoln's draft of the Preliminary Proclamation of Emancipation, September, 1862.

From the original in the Library of the State of New York, Albany.

therefore, that the actors in this new drama
of reconstruction played their parts awk-
wardly and with many mistakes.

A most interesting constitutional problem
had to be faced at the outset : What effect
had secession had upon the States guilty of
it ; was it or was it not an act of state
suicide ?   This question was warmly de-
bated in Congress and out.   Although
ridiculed in some quarters as a mere
metaphysical quibble, it lay at the bottom
of men's political thinking on reconstruction, and their views of the proper answer
to it powerfully influenced their action.

All loyal Democrats and most Republicans answered it in the negative.   Secession, they said, being an invalid act, had
no effect whatever ; the rebellious tracts
were still States of the Union in spite of
themselves.   But the two parties reasoned
their way to this conclusion by different
roads.   The Democrats deduced the view
from the State's intrinsic sovereignty, the
Republicans from the national Constitution
as ordaining "an indestructible Union of

indestructible States." This class of thinkers, in whichever party they were found,
naturally preferred the term "restoration"
to "reconstruction."

The theory of state suicide was held by
many, but with a difference. Sumner and
a few others deemed that secession had
destroyed statehood alone; that over individuals the Constitution still extended its
authority and its protection, as in Territories. Thaddeus Stevens and his followers
viewed secession as having left the State
not only defunct but a washed slate govern-
mentally, like soil won by conquest. Both
these parties conceived the work before
Congress to be out-and-out "reconstruction," involving the right to change old
state lines and institutions at will. Not
even this position was more ultra than the
course which reconstruction actually took.

Closely related to this main problem
were several other questions nearly or quite
as vexing. Were any conditions to be imposed upon the peoples seeking re-admission to the Union as States? If so, what.

aside from the loyalty of voters and office-holders, were these conditions? Was the President to initiate and oversee the process of redintegration, prescribing the conditions of re-admission, and determining when they were fulfilled, or was all this the business of Congress? And, lastly, did the right thus to oversee and impose conditions depend upon a certain war power of Congress or of President, or upon the clause of the Constitution which guarantees to every State a republican form of government? Nearly the same question as this, in another form, would be, Was this right explicitly constitutional or only impliedly so?

The answer practically returned to these difficult inquiries was that Congress, as a *quasi* war right, must exact of the States lately in secession all the conditions necessary, in its view, to their permanent loyalty and the peace of the Union.

The history of reconstruction divides into three periods: Reconstruction during the war, President Johnson's work, and Congressional reconstruction.

Restoration was the universal thought at first. Congressional resolutions in 1861 declared that the war was not waged "for the purpose of overthrowing or interfering with the rights or established institutions" of the seceding States. Their action was looked upon as an insurrection against the state government as well as against the United States. Accordingly, when a handful of Virginia loyalists, in the summer of 1861, formed a state government and elected national senators and representatives, President and Congress recognized them as the true State of Virginia.

Following out the same idea, President Lincoln proclaimed in 1863 that as soon as one-tenth of the voters of any seceded State would swear to abide by the Constitution and the emancipation laws they might form a state government. In this way Louisiana, Arkansas, and Tennessee were reconstructed during 1863 and 1865.

The hand of the assassin removed Lincoln from the scene of action at a time when North and South alike stood most in need of his kind heart, tact, and firmness. Andrew Johnson succeeded to a task for which he was ill-fitted. Conceited, obstinate, and pugnacious, he began by alarming the South with threats of wholesale punishment for the " crime of treason," and ended by alienating his own party through his slack methods of re-establishing the States. Johnson declared, and no doubt honestly, that he was carrying out Lincoln's ideas. In May, 1865, he offered amnesty to all but certain excepted classes, mainly civil and military leaders, upon condition of an oath to support the Constitution, including its Thirteenth Amendment, forbidding slavery. Though the proclamation declaring this to be in force did not issue till December 18, 1865, it had been approved by Congress the preceding February.

President Johnson then proceeded to reorganize the state governments. For each seceded State, except the four already reconstructed, he appointed a provincial governor. The governor called a State convention. Only whites who had taken the amnesty oath could elect delegates, or themselves be elected, to this convention. At the instance of the President the convention adopted a constitution or legislation which forbade slavery, declared the ordinance of secession null and void, and repudiated the Confederate debt. The convention then appointed times and places for the election of a legislature and a permanent governor. In a few months the governmental machinery had been set in motion in all the late Confederate States, and in December senators and representatives from all except Texas were knocking at the doors of Congress.

Thus far the President had had full sway. But upon the re-assembling of Congress in December, it became apparent that he and his party were not in harmony. Congress, still overwhelmingly republican, refused to admit the southern delegates, and appointed a committee to investigate the condition of affairs in the southern States. Its report was anything but re-assuring, and Congress, mainly under the lead of Thaddeus Stevens, boldly proceeded to rip up the entire presidential work.

Several considerations led Congress to this course. They denied the President's right, on his own sole authority, to re-establish permanent governments in the States in question. Furthermore, the new state governments were declared unlawful because their constitutions had not been submitted to the people for ratification. Congress also maintained that only the law-making power could of right determine the conditions of re-admission to the Union, and judge whether or not those conditions had been fulfilled.

But the consideration which outweighed all others in favor of the congressional procedure was the alarming temper and acts of the South itself. The Carolinas and Georgia had simply repealed the ordinance of secession instead of declaring it null and void. The reconstructed legislatures pensioned Confederate soldiers and their families. "Notorious and unpardoned rebels" were elected as state officers and to Congress.

Worse than this, nearly all the southern States passed laws which went far toward reducing the blacks again to slavery. In Virginia, if a negro broke his labor-contract, the employer could pursue him and compel him to work an extra month, with chain and ball if necessary. In Mississippi negro children who were orphans, or whose parents did not support them, were to be apprenticed till they became of age. Their masters could inflict upon them "moderate corporal punishment," and re-capture such as ran away. In South Carolina any negro engaging in business had to pay one hundred dollars yearly as a license. Mechanics were fined ten dollars each a year for prosecuting their trades. No negro could settle in the State without giving bonds for his good behavior and support. In Louisiana a farm laborer was required to make a year's contract; if he failed to work out the time, he could be punished by forced labor upon public works. Not all the new southern legislation was of this savage character, and this itself must be viewed in the light of the fact that the negroes, trained in irresponsibility, were inclined to idleness and theft. But it was nevertheless unjust. In some sections only the interposition of the military and of the Freedman's Bureau made life tolerable to the blacks.

As an offset to the above dangerous acts and tendencies, Congress, in the spring of 1866, passed the Fourteenth Amendment [1] and submitted it to the States for ratification. It was meant to insure to negroes in every State all the rights of citizens and the equal protection of the laws. If and so long as negroes were in any State forbidden to vote, it reduced that State's representation in Congress proportionally; it excluded from national and state offices certain specified Confederate leaders; and it guarded the national debt, repudiating all indebtedness on behalf of the Rebellion. Every secession State but Tennessee rejected the amendment.

Congress replied by the "iron law" of

[1] Declared in force July 28, 1868, having been ratified by three-fourths of the States.

March 2, 1867. "Secessia" was divided into five districts and placed under military rule, there to remain until certain conditions were fulfilled. These conditions were, in brief, the calling of a state convention by the loyal citizens, blacks included; the framing by the convention of a constitution enfranchising negroes; the ratification of this constitution by the people and its approval by Congress; the ratification of the Fourteenth Amendment by the new legislature. Having conformed to these prescriptions the State might be represented in Congress and consider itself fully restored to the Union. A supplementary law of March 19th hastened the process by giving the district commanders surveillance of registration and the initiative in calling conventions.

By June, 1868, a sufficient number of the southern States had complied with the conditions to make the Fourteenth Amendment law. Virginia, Mississippi, and Texas held out till 1870, and hence were forced to ratify the Fifteenth Amendment also. Not

till January 30, 1871, were all the States
again represented in both Houses of Congress as in 1860.

All through the days of congressional

Edwin M. Stanton.

reconstruction the antagonism between
President and Congress steadily increased.
Every step in the progress encountered the
President's uttermost opposition and spite.
He vetoed all important reconstruction
measures, which were promptly carried over

his veto. There was much violent language and bitter feeling on both sides. The irritation finally culminated when the House entered articles of impeachment against Johnson—the only case of the kind in our history involving a President. The charges were tried before the Senate in March, 1868, the Chief Justice presiding, and occupied three weeks. William M. Evarts was Johnson's counsel, and a glittering array of legal talent appeared on both sides. The main charge was that the President had wilfully violated the Tenure of Office Act in removing Secretary Stanton from the Cabinet after the Senate had once refused to concur in his removal. The House was hasty in bringing the prosecution. The President was acquitted by a vote of 19 against and 35 for impeachment—one vote less than the two-thirds necessary to impeach. The Johnson-Congressional conflict proved one of the most mortifying episodes in our country's history.

Ulysses S. Grant.

PERIOD V.

THE CEMENTED UNION

1868–1888

CHAPTER I.

POLITICAL HISTORY OF THE LAST TWO DECADES

THE presidential election of 1868 was decided at Appomattox. General Grant was borne to the White House on a flood-tide of popularity, carrying twenty-six out of the thirty-four voting States. Schuyler Colfax, of Indiana, became Vice-President. The Democrats had nominated Horatio Seymour, of New York, and F. P. Blair, of Missouri. Reconstruction was the great issue. The democratic platform demanded universal amnesty and the immediate restoration of all the commonwealths lately in secession, and insisted that the regulation of the franchise should be left with States.

The management of the South was the most serious problem before the new administration. The whites were striving by fair means and foul to get political power back into their own hands. The reconstructed state governments, dependent upon black majorities, were too weak for successful resistance. The Ku-Klux and similar organizations were practically a masked army. The President was appealed to for military aid, and he responded. Small detachments of United States troops hurried hither and thither. Wherever they appeared resistance ceased ; but when fresh outbreaks elsewhere called the soldiers away, the fight against the hated state government was immediately renewed. The negroes soon learned to stay at home on election day, and the whites, once in the saddle, were too skilful riders to be thrown.

Congress, meanwhile, still strongly republican, was taking active measures to protect the blacks. In 1870 it passed an act imposing fines and damages for a conspiracy to deprive negroes of the suffrage. The Force Act of 1871 was a much harsher measure. It empowered the President to employ the army, navy, and militia to suppress combinations which deprived the negro of the rights guaranteed him by the Fourteenth Amendment. For such combinations to appear in arms was made rebellion against the United States, and the President might suspend *habeas corpus* in the rebellious district. By President Grant, in the fall of 1871, this was actually done in parts of the Carolinas. State registrations and elections were to be supervised by United States marshals, who could command the help of the United States military or naval forces.

The Force Act outran popular feeling. It came dangerously near the practical suspension of state government in the South, and many at the North, including some Republicans, thought the latter result a greater evil than even the temporary abeyance of negro suffrage. The " Liberal Republicans " bolted. In 1872 they nomi-

nated Horace Greeley for the Presidency,
and adopted a platform declaring local self-
government a better safeguard for the
rights of all citizens than centralized power.
The platform also protested against the
supremacy of the military over the civil
power and the suspension of . *habeas corpus*,
and favored universal amnesty to men at
the South.   Charles Sumner, Stanley Mat-
thews, Carl Schurz, David A. Wells, and
many other prominent Republicans engaged
in the opposition.

Thinking their opportunity had come, the
Democrats indorsed the Liberals' platform
and nominees.   The Republicans renom-
inated Grant by acclamation, and joined
with him on the ticket Henry Wilson, of
Massachusetts.

As the campaign went on, the Greeley
movement developed remarkable strength
and remarkable weakness.   Speaking for
years through the New York *Tribune*, Mr.
Greeley had won, in a remarkable degree,
the respect and even the affection of the
country.   His offer to give bail for Jeffer-

son Davis in his imprisonment, and his stanch advocacy of mercy to all who had engaged in secession, so soon as they had grounded arms, made him hosts of friends even in the South. He took the stump himself, making the tour of Pennsylvania, Ohio, and Indiana, and crowds of Republicans came to see and hear their former champion.

But the Democrats could not heartily unite in the support of such a lifelong and bitter opponent of their party. Some supported a third ticket, while many others did not vote at all. Mr. Greeley, too, an ardent protectionist, was not popular with the influential free-trade element among the Liberals themselves. The election resulted in a sweeping victory for the republican ticket. The Democrats carried but six States, and those were all in the South. Within a month after the election, Mr. Greeley died, broken down by over-exertion, family bereavement, and disappointed ambition.

Troubles in the South continued during

Grant's second term. The turmoil reached
its height in Louisiana in 1874. Ever since
1872 the whites in that State had been
chafing under republican rule. The election of Governor Kellogg was disputed,
and he was accused of having plunged the
State into ruinous debt. In August, 1874,
a disturbance occurred which ended in the
deliberate shooting of six republican officials. President Grant prepared to send
military aid to the Kellogg government.
Thereupon Penn, the defeated candidate
for Lieutenant-governor in 1872, issued an
address to the people, claiming to be the
lawful executive of Louisiana, and calling
upon the state militia to arm and drive
"the usurpers from power." Barricades
were thrown up in the streets of New
Orleans, and on September 14th a severe
fight took place between the insurgents
and the state forces, in which a dozen were
killed on each side. On the next day the
state-house was surrendered to the militia,
ten thousand of whom had responded to
Penn's call. Governor Kellogg took refuge

in the custom-house.   Penn was formally
inducted into office.   United States troops
were hurried to the scene.   Agreeably to
their professions of loyalty toward the
Federal Government, the insurgents surrendered the state property to the United
States authorities without resistance, but
under protest.   The Kellogg government
was re-instated.

Troops at the polls secured quiet in the
November elections.   The returning board
decided that the Republicans had elected
their governor and fifty-four members of
the legislature.   Fifty-two members were
democratic, while the election of five members remained in doubt, and was left to the
decision of the legislature.   The Democrats
vehemently protested against the decision
of the returning board, claiming an all-
round victory.   Fearing trouble at the as-
sembling of the legislature in January, 1875,
President Grant placed General Sheridan in
command at New Orleans.   The legislature
met on January 4th.   Our reports of what
followed are conflicting.   The admitted

facts are that the democratic members, law-fully or unlawfully, placed a speaker in the chair. Some disorder ensuing, United States soldiers were called in and, at the request of the democratic speaker, restored quiet. The Republicans meanwhile had left the house. The Democrats then elected members to fill the five seats left vacant by the returning board. Later in the day, United States troops, under orders from Governor Kellogg, to whom the re-publican legislators had appealed, ejected the five new members. The Republicans re-entered the house, and the Democrats thereupon withdrew. Subsequently a con-gressional committee made unsuccessful attempts to settle the dispute. The demo-cratic members finally returned, and a sullen acquiescence in the Kellogg gov-ernment gradually prevailed.

By 1876 every southern State was solidly democratic except Louisiana, South Caro-lina, and Florida, and in these republican governments were upheld only by the bayonet.

The presidential election of 1876 was a
contest of general tendencies rather than
of definite principles. The opposing parties were more nearly matched than they
had been since 1860. The Democrats
nominated Samuel J. Tilden, of New York,
and Thomas A. Hendricks, of Indiana.
Rutherford B. Hayes, of Ohio, and William
A. Wheeler, of New York, became the
republican standard-bearers. The election
passed off quietly, troops being stationed
at the polls in turbulent quarters. Mr.
Tilden carried New York, New Jersey,
Indiana, and Connecticut. With a solid
South, he had won the day. But the returning boards of Louisiana, Florida, and
South Carolina, throwing out the votes of
several democratic districts on the ground
of fraud or intimidation, decided that those
States had gone republican, giving Hayes
a majority of one in the electoral college.
The Democrats raised the cry of fraud.
Suppressed excitement pervaded the coun-
try. Threats were even muttered that
Hayes would never be inaugurated. Presi-

dent Grant quietly strengthened the military force in and about Washington. The country looked to Congress for a peaceful solution of the problem, and not in vain.

The Constitution provides that " the President of the Senate shall, in presence of the Senate and House of Representatives, open all the [electoral] certificates, and the votes shall then be counted." Certain Republicans held that the power to count the votes lay with the President of the Senate, the House and Senate being mere spectators. The Democrats naturally objected to this construction, since Mr. Ferry, the republican president of the Senate, could then count the votes of the disputed States for Hayes.

The Democrats insisted that Congress should continue the practice followed since 1865, which was that no vote objected to should be counted except by the concurrence of both houses. The House was strongly democratic; by throwing out the vote of one State it could elect Tilden.

The deadlock could be broken only by a

Samuel J. Tilden.

After a pastel by Sarony in the house at Gramercy Park.

compromise. A joint committee reported the famous Electoral Commission Bill, which passed House and Senate by large majorities; 186 Democrats voting for the bill and 18 against it, while the republican vote stood 52 for and 75 against. The bill created a commission of five senators, five representatives, and five justices of the United States Supreme Court, the fifth justice being chosen by the four appointed in the bill. Previous to this choice the commission contained seven Democrats and seven Republicans. It was expected that the fifth justice would be Hon. David Davis, of Illinois, a neutral with democratic leanings; but his unexpected election as democratic senator from his State caused Justice Bradley to be selected to the post of decisive umpire. The votes of all disputed States were to be submitted to the commission for decision.

It was drawing perilously near to inauguration day. The commission met on the last day of January. The cases of Florida, Louisiana, Oregon, and South Carolina

were in succession submitted to it by
Congress. Eminent counsel appeared for
each side. There were double sets of returns from every one of the States named.
In the three southern States the governor
recognized by the United States had signed
the republican certificates. The democratic
certificates from Florida were signed by the
state attorney-general and the new democratic governor; those from Louisiana by
the democratic gubernatorial candidate, who
claimed to be the lawful governor; those
from South Carolina by no state official,
the Tilden electors simply claiming to
have been chosen by the popular vote
and rejected by the returning board. In
Oregon the democratic governor declared
one of the Hayes electors ineligible because an office-holder, and gave a certificate to Cronin, the highest Tilden elector,
instead. The other two Hayes electors refused to recognize Cronin, and, associating
with them the rejected republican elector,
presented a certificate signed by the secretary of state. Cronin, appointing two

new electors to act with him, cast his vote for Tilden, his associates voting for Hayes. This certificate was signed by the governor and attested by the secretary of state.

After deciding not to go behind any returns which were *prima facie* lawful, the commission, by a strict party vote of eight to seven, gave a decision for the Hayes electors in every case. March 2d it adjourned, and three days later Hayes was inaugurated without disturbance.

The whole country heaved a sigh of relief. All agreed that provision must be made against such peril in the future ; but it was not till late in 1886 that Congress could agree upon the necessary measure. The Electoral Count Bill was then passed, and signed by the President on February 3, 1887. It aims to throw upon each State, so far as possible, the responsibility of determining how its own presidential vote has been cast. It provides that the President of the Senate shall open the electoral certificates in the presence of both houses, and hand them to the tellers, two from each house, who are to read them aloud and record the votes.

If there has been no dispute as to the list of electors from a State, such list, where certified in due form, is to be accepted as a matter of course. In case of dispute, the procedure is as follows : If but one set of returns appears and this is authenticated by a state electoral tribunal constituted to settle the dispute, such returns shall be conclusive. If there are two or more sets of returns, the set approved by the state tribunal shall be accepted. If there are two rival tribunals, the vote of the State shall be thrown out, unless both houses, acting separately, agree upon the lawful- ness of one tribunal or the other. If there has been no decision by a tribunal, those votes shall be counted which both houses, acting separately, decide to be lawful. If the houses disagree, the votes certified to by the governor shall be accepted.

President Hayes's first important action was the withdrawal of troops from South

Carolina and Louisiana, where the rival
governments existed side by side. The
republican governments at once fell to the
ground. As the Democrats had already
got control in Florida, the "solid South"
was now an accomplished fact. Financial
questions were those which chiefly occupied the public mind during Hayes's administration. They are referred to in Chapter
VII., below.

Returning from a remarkable tour around
the world, General Grant became in 1880 a
candidate for a third-term nomination. The
deadlock in the republican convention between him and Mr. Blaine was broken by
the nomination of James A. Garfield, of
Ohio. Chester A. Arthur, of New York,
was the vice-presidential candidate. The
Democrats nominated the hero of Gettysburg, the brave and renowned General
W. S. Hancock, of Pennsylvania, and
William H. English, of Indiana. Garfield
was elected, receiving 214 electoral votes
against 155 for Hancock. Hancock carried
every southern State; Garfield every north-

ern State except New Jersey, Nevada, and California.

President Garfield had hardly entered upon his high duties when he was cut down by the hand of an assassin. On the morning of July 2, 1881, the President entered the railway station at Washington, intending to take an eastern trip. Charles J. Guiteau, a disappointed office-seeker, crept up behind him and fired two bullets at him, one of which lodged in his back. The President died on September 19th, after weeks of suffering. Vice-President Arthur succeeded to the presidency, and had an uneventful but respectable administration.

Guiteau's trial began in November and lasted more than two months. The defence was insanity. The assassin maintained that he was inspired to commit the deed, and that it was a political necessity. The "stalwart" Republicans, headed by Senator Conkling, had quarrelled with the President over certain appointments unacceptable to the New York senator; Guiteau pretended to think the removal of Mr.

James A. Garfield.

Garfield necessary to the unity of the party and the salvation of the country. The prosecution showed that Guiteau had long been an unprincipled adventurer, greedy for notoriety; that he first conceived of killing the President after his hopes of office were finally destroyed; and that he had planned the murder several weeks in advance. Guiteau was found guilty, and executed at Washington on June 30, 1882. The autopsy showed no disease of the brain.

Although it had no logical connection with the "spoils" system, the assassination of President Garfield called the attention of the whole country to the crying need of reform in the civil service. Ever since the days of President Jackson, in 1829, appointments to the minor federal offices had been used for the payment of party debts and to keep up partisan interest. This practice incurred the deep condemnation of Webster, Clay, Calhoun, and others, but no practical steps toward reform were taken till 1871. The abuses of the spoils system

had then become so flagrant that Congress
created a civil service commission, which
instituted competitive examinations to test
the merits of candidates for office in the
departments at Washington.   President
Grant reported that the new methods
"had given persons of superior capacity
to the service."   But Congress, always
niggardly in its appropriations for the
work of the commission, after 1875 cut
them off altogether, and the rules were
suspended.

Under President Hayes civil service
reform made considerable progress in an
irregular way.   Secretary Schurz enforced
competitive examinations in the Interior
department.   They were also applied by
Mr. James to the New York Post-office,
and, as the result, one-third more work was
done with less cost.   Similar good results
followed the enforcement of the "merit
system" in the New York custom-house
after 1879.   President Hayes also strongly
condemned political assessments upon office-
holders, but with small practical effect.

The alarming increase of corruption in political circles generally, after the war, helped to create popular sentiment for reform. Corrupt "rings" sprang up in every city. The "whiskey ring," composed of distillers and government employees, assumed national proportions in 1874, cheating the Government out of a large part of its revenue from spirits. Liberal appropriations for building a navy were squandered.

During the campaign of 1872, the Democrats charged several prominent Congressmen with having taken bribes, in 1867–68, to vote for legislation desired by the Union Pacific Railroad. At the request of the accused, an examination was had by a House committee. The committee's report in 1873 recommended the expulsion of Representatives Oakes Ames and James Brooks. Mr. Ames was accused of selling to Congressmen at reduced rates, with intent to influence their votes, shares of stock in the "Crédit Mobilier," a corporation for the construction of the Union

Pacific Railroad.   Mr. Brooks, who was a
government director in the railroad, was
charged with receiving such shares.   The
House did not expel the two members,
but severely condemned them.   Shadows
of varying density fell upon many prominent politicians and darkened their subsequent careers.

The tragic fate of President Garfield,
following these and other revelations of
political corruption, brought public sentiment on civil service reform to a head.   A
bill prepared by the Civil Service Reform
League, and introduced by Senator Pendleton, of Ohio, passed Congress in January,
1883, and on the 16th received the signa-
ture of the President.

It authorized the President, with the
consent of the Senate, to appoint three
civil service commissioners, who were to
institute competitive examinations open to
all persons desiring to enter the government employ.   It provided that the clerks
in the departments at Washington, and in
every customs district or post-office where

James G. Blaine.

fifty or more were employed, should be arranged in classes, and that in the future only persons who had passed the examinations should be appointed to service in these offices or promoted from a lower class to a higher, preference being given according to rank in the examinations. Candidates were to serve six months' probation at practical work before receiving a final appointment. The bill struck a heavy blow at political assessments, by declaring that no official should be removed for refusing to contribute to political funds. Congressmen or government officials convicted of soliciting or receiving political assessments from government employees became liable to a five thousand dollar fine, or three years' imprisonment, or both. Persons in the government service were forbidden to use their official authority or influence to coerce the political action of any one, or to interfere with elections.

Dorman B. Eaton, Leroy B. Thoman, and John M. Gregory were appointed

commissioners by President Arthur. By
the end of the year the new system was
fairly in operation. Besides the departments at Washington, it applied to eleven
customs districts and twenty-three post-
offices where fifty or more officials were
employed. The law could be thoroughly
tested only when a new party came into
power; that time was near at hand.

The deepest and most significant political movement of the last twenty years has
been the gradual recovery of power by the
Democracy. For some years after the
Rebellion, this party's war record was a
millstone around its neck. The financial
distress in 1873 and the corruption prevalent in political circles weakened the party
in power, while the Democracy, putting
slavery and reconstruction behind its back,
turned to new issues, and raised the cry
of "economy" and "reform."

The state elections of 1874 witnessed a
"tidal wave" of democratic victories. Out
of 292 members of the House in 1875, 198
were democratic. Two-thirds of the Sena-

tors were still republican.   Even by republican reckoning, the democratic presidential
ticket in 1876 received a popular majority
of 157,000 and lacked but one electoral
vote.   In 1879 both houses of Congress
were democratic, by small majorities, for
the first time since 1856.   The tide ebbed
in 1880, the Democrats losing control of
the House, and suffering a decisive defeat
in the presidential election; but with 1884
the fortune of the Democracy reached high-
water mark.

In this year James G. Blaine, of Maine,
and John A. Logan, of Illinois, received the
republican nomination for President and
Vice-President.   A number of Independent
Republicans, including the most earnest
advocates of civil service reform, were
strongly opposed to Mr. Blaine, alleging
him to be personally corrupt and the rep-
resentative of corrupt political methods.
They met in conference, denounced the
nominations, and later indorsed the democratic nominees—Grover Cleveland, governor of New York, and Thomas A.

Hendricks, of Indiana. George W. Curtis, Carl Schurz, and other prominent Republicans took part in the movement. Several influential Independent Republican papers, including the New York *Times*, Boston *Herald*, and Springfield *Republican*, joined the bolt.

The campaign was bitterly personal, attacks upon the characters of the candidates taking the place of a discussion of principles. Mr. Cleveland was elected, receiving 219 electoral votes against 182 for Mr. Blaine. He carried every southern State, besides New York, Connecticut, Indiana, Delaware, Maryland, and New Jersey. The total popular vote was over 10,000,000 —the largest ever cast. Cleveland had 4,911,000, a plurality of 62,000 over Blaine. The Democrats regained control of the House in 1883, and held it by a considerable majority to the end of Mr. Cleveland's first term. In the Senate, until the election of 1892, the Republicans continued to have a small majority.

Upon the accession of the new adminis-

President Grover Cleveland.

tration to power, the country waited with deep interest to see its effect upon the civil service. Mr. Cleveland had pledged himself to a rigid enforcement of the new law, and encouraged all to believe that with him impartial civil service would not be confined to the few offices thus protected. After the first few months of Cleveland's administration, one fact was apparent : for the first time since the days of Jackson a change of the party in power had not been followed by a clean sweep among the holders of offices. But, as the subsequent record painfully shows, office-holders' pressure proved too strong for Mr. Cleveland's resolution.

There were then about 120,000 government employees. Of these, not far from 14,000 were covered by the Pendleton law. All the other minor places were held at the pleasure of superior officers. These latter officers numbered about 58,000. In August, 1887, from 45,000 to 48,000 of them had been changed, implying change in the offices dependent upon them. There were

some 55,000 postmasters, 2,400 of whom
were appointed by the President for a term
of four years, the rest by the postmaster-
general at pleasure. At the date named,
from 37,000 to 47,000 changes had been
made in this department. These changes,
of course, were not all removals, as many
vacancies occur by expiration of terms,
death of incumbents, and other causes.

An important statute regarding the presidential succession, introduced by Senator
Hoar, passed Congress in January, 1886.
By previous statutes, in case of the removal, death, resignation, or disability of
the President and Vice-President, the
presidency passed in order to the temporary President of the Senate and the
Speaker of the House. The latter two
might be of the opposite party from the
President's, so that by the succession of
either the will of the people as expressed
in the presidential election would mani-
festly be defeated. Moreover, in case of
a President's death and the accession of
the Vice-President, the latter, too, might

die, and thus both the presidency and
the vice-presidency become vacant in the
interim between two Congresses, when
there is neither President of the Senate
nor Speaker of the House. Thus President Garfield died September 19, 1881,
and the XLVIIIth Congress did not con-
vene to choose a Speaker until the next
December. The Senate had adjourned
without electing a presiding officer. Had
President Arthur died at any moment
during the intervening period—and it is
said that he was for a time in imminent
danger of death—the distracting contin-
gency just spoken of would have been
upon the country.

According to the new law, in case of a
vacancy in both presidency and vice-presidency, the presidency devolves upon the
members of the cabinet in the historical
order of the establishment of their departments, beginning with the Secretary of
State. Should he die, be impeached, or
disabled, the Secretary of the Treasury
would become President, to be followed

in like crisis by the Secretary of War, he by the Attorney-General, he by the Post-master-General, he by the Secretary of the Navy, he by the Secretary of the Interior, and he by the Secretary of Agriculture. We have still no legal or official criterion of a President's disability.   We do not know whether, during Garfield's illness, for instance—apparently a clear case of disability—it was proper for his cabinet to perform his presidential duties, or whether Arthur should not have assumed these.   Barring this chance for conflict, it is not easy to think of an emergency in which the chief magistracy can now fall vacant, or the appropriate incumbent thereof be in doubt.

CHAPTER II.

THE TREATY OF WASHINGTON

THE year 1871 was marked by the conclusion of an important treaty between
England and the United States. Besides
settling certain questions which threatened
the friendly relations of the two countries,
the treaty enunciated important principles
of international law, and afforded the world
a shining instance of peaceful arbitration
as a substitute for the horrors of war.

Ever since 1863 the United States had
been seeking satisfaction from Great Britain for the depredations committed by the
Alabama and other Confederate cruisers
sailing from English ports. Negotiations
were broken off in 1865 and again in 1868.
The next year Reverdy Johnson, American
Minister to England, negotiated a treaty,
but it was rejected by the Senate. In

January, 1871, the British Government proposed a joint commission for the settlement
of questions connected with the Canadian
fisheries. Mr. Fish, our Secretary of State,
replied that the settlement of the "Alabama Claims" would be "essential to the
restoration of cordial and amicable relations
between the two governments." England
consented to submit this question also to
the commission, and on February 27th five
high commissioners from each country met
at Washington. The British delegation
included cabinet officers, the minister to the
United States, and an Oxford professor of
international law. The American commissioners were of equally high station, the
Secretary of State, an associate justice of
the Supreme Court, and our minister to
England being of their number.

On May 8th the commission completed a
treaty which was speedily ratified by both
governments. It provided for arbitration
upon the "Alabama Claims," upon other
claims by citizens of either country for
damages during the Rebellion, upon the

fisheries, and upon the northwest boundary
of the United States.   Provisions were also
made by it for the common use of the lakes,
rivers, and canals along the Canadian border, and for the transit of merchandise free
of duty, under certain conditions, across
either country to and from certain ports.

The fisheries part of the treaty is dis-
cussed in the next chapter.   The question
of the northwest boundary was referred to
the decision of the German emperor, William I.   The treaty of 1846 had left it
doubtful whether the boundary line through
the channel between Vancouver Island
and the main-land should be so run as to
include the island of San Juan, with its
group, in the United States or in Canada.
The emperor's decision, given in 1872, was
in favor of the United States.

Three commissioners—one appointed by
each government and a third appointed
jointly—met in Washington, September 26,
1871, to pass judgment upon the war claims
other than the "Alabama Claims."   The
American claims of this class, amounting to

less than $1,000,000, were all rejected on
the ground that the British Government was
not proved responsible for the damages
incurred.   British subjects put in claims for
$96,000,000.   The commission allowed less
than $2,000,000, which the United States
Government promptly paid into the British
treasury.

But far the most important and interesting part of the treaty was the provision for
the settlement of the "Alabama Claims."
England's unfriendly attitude during the
war and her subsequent refusal to submit
the "claims" to arbitration, had stirred up
much hard feeling throughout the United
States.   The graceful expression, in the
preamble to the treaty, of England's regret
for the ravages of the cruisers was therefore very gratifying.   More material satisfaction was to follow.   The treaty provided
that the claims should be submitted to a
tribunal of five persons—one appointed by
each government and one each by the
Emperor of Brazil, the President of Switzerland, and the King of Italy.

The tribunal met at Geneva, Switzerland, December 15, 1871. Charles Francis Adams, our minister to England during the war, was the United States member, and Lord Chief Justice Cockburn the English. Baron Itajuba, the Brazilian minister plenipotentiary to France, Count Sclopis, an Italian minister of State, and M. Jaques Stæmpfli, of Switzerland, comprised the rest of the tribunal. Each side was represented by counsel, Caleb Cushing, William M. Evarts, and Morrison R. Waite appearing for the United States. An agent presented the printed case of each government.

The American claims included direct and indirect losses—direct, by the destruction of vessels with their cargoes and by national expenditure in chasing the Confederate cruisers ; indirect, by the loss of a large part of the United States ocean carrying trade, by increased marine insurance rates, and by the prolongation of the war with proportionally increased expense. Great Britain vehemently objected to the indirect claims coming before the tribunal, and at one time seemed about to withdraw. Upon reassembling in June, 1872, the tribunal decided that the indirect claims were not admissible, and the case went forward. Counsel having presented their respective arguments, the tribunal took up the case of each cruiser separately. During the consideration of damages it sat with closed doors, only the arbitrators being present. On September 14th, after thirty-two conferences, the tribunal gave its decision.

The Geneva case is of two-fold interest, first, for its decision of the facts involved, and the consequent award; second, for its enunciation of important principles of international law.

The Treaty of Washington laid down three rules for the guidance of the tribunal. They are such important contributions to international law that they must be quoted in full.

"A neutral government is bound,

"First: To use due diligence to prevent the fitting out, arming or equipping, within its jurisdiction, of any vessel which it has reasonable ground to believe is intended to cruise or to carry on war against a power with which it is at peace, and also to use like diligence to prevent the departure from its jurisdiction of any vessel intended to cruise or carry on war as above, such vessel having been specially adapted, in whole or in part, within such jurisdiction, to warlike use.

"Secondly: Not to permit or suffer either belligerent to make use of its ports or waters as the base of naval operations against the other, or for the purpose of the renewal or augmentation of military supplies or arms, or the recruitment of men.

"Thirdly: To exercise due diligence in its own ports and waters, and as to all persons within its jurisdiction, to prevent any violation of the foregoing obligations and duties."

Great Britain denied, in the text of the treaty, that these rules were a true statement of the principles of international law in force during the Rebellion, but consented that the "Alabama Claims" should be decided in accordance with them. Both countries also agreed to abide by them in future and to invite other maritime powers to do the same.

Questions being raised by the counsel as to the interpretation of certain terms and the scope of certain provisions in the three rules, the tribunal found it necessary to make the following preliminary decisions :

1. The meaning of "due diligence." The tribunal took the ground that what constitutes "due diligence" varies with the circumstances of the case. The greater the probable damage to either belligerent, the greater must be the care taken by the neutral government to prevent the escape of cruisers from its ports.

2. Should a neutral detain an escaped cruiser when it re-enters the neutral's jurisdiction, the cruiser having in the meantime been regularly commissioned by its government ? The arbitrators decided that

the neutral had a right to detain such a
cruiser, in spite of its commission, but was
under no positive obligation to do so.

3. Does a neutral's responsibility end
with the enforcement of its local laws to
prevent the escape of cruisers, even if those
laws are inadequate? Decision was given
that the case must be determined by international law and not by national legislation.
If a country's regulations for carrying out
its acknowledged international duties are
ineffective, they ought to be changed.

These decisions in international law,
coming from so exalted a source, were of
world-wide significance. The verdict on
the facts in the case had, however, more
immediate interest for the two contestants.

The American case claimed damages for
losses inflicted by fourteen cruisers and
four tenders. The award allowed for only
the Alabama with her tender, the Florida
with her three tenders, and the Shenandoah
during a part of her career. With regard
to the Alabama the culpability of the British Government was so clearly shown that

even the English arbitrator voted in favor of the American claim. The Florida was permitted to escape from Liverpool although Mr. Adams, the United States minister, repeatedly called the attention of the authorities to her notorious warlike character. The vessel was, furthermore, libelled at Nassau, a British colonial port, but the British officials allowed her to take in supplies and put to sea. The Shenandoah set sail from Liverpool with the connivance of the Government, received her armament at the Madeira Islands, and after a destructive career was welcomed at the British port of Melbourne, repaired in a government slip, and furnished with supplies and recruits. The award held Great Britain responsible only for her career after leaving Melbourne.

The American case further claimed damages for national expense in chasing the cruisers, and for the prospective earnings of the lost merchantmen, but these claims, along with those explicitly denounced as indirect, were rejected.

The tribunal awarded $15,500,000 damages in gold for the vessels and cargoes destroyed by the three cruisers and their tenders. Of this sum, about $2,000,000 was interest at six per cent. The only dissenting voice was that of the British member, who submitted a long and able, but somewhat spiteful, minority report.

The award naturally gave great satisfaction in the United States. The money compensation was in itself a source of considerable gratulation ; but the fact that stiff-backed England had by a clearly impartial tribunal of the highest character been declared in the wrong was not the least pleasurable side of the result. American citizens should never forget the services, in this delicate and difficult matter, of Mr. Adams. By his great knowledge of law, his careful gathering of evidence, and his brave, sturdy and incessant, though apparently useless, remonstrances with the British authorities while the cruisers were building and their depredations going on, he established a case which could not be gainsaid. Hardly had he opened his portfolio at Geneva when the learned arbitrators saw that his suit must be allowed.

England promptly handed over to the United States the price of her sympathy with rebellion and slavery. The course of Congress in dealing with the award was not very creditable. For four years the money lay in the treasury vaults, piling up interest at five per cent. until it amounted to $20,000,000. A Court of Alabama Claims was then convened, where private claimants might press their suits. Insurance companies which could show that their losses on vessels destroyed by the cruisers exceeded the premiums received, were entitled to be paid the difference, with interest at four per cent.

CHAPTER III.

OUR glance at the Treaty of Washington introduces us to an international complication which has been transmitted from the very birthday of the nation, and is, alas, still unsettled, spite of the earnest efforts to this end made since 1885. Article 3 of the treaty of 1783 was as follows: "It is agreed that the people of the United States shall continue to enjoy unmolested the right to take fish of every kind on the Grand Bank and on all the other banks of Newfoundland; also in the Gulf of St. Lawrence and at all other places in the sea where the inhabitants of both countries used at any time heretofore to fish; and also that the inhabitants of the United States shall have liberty to take fish of every kind on such part of the

coast of Newfoundland as British fishermen shall use [but not to dry or cure
the same on that island]; and also on the
coasts, bays, and creeks of all other of his
Britannic Majesty's dominions in America,
and that the American fishermen shall have
liberty to dry and cure fish in any of the
unsettled bays, harbors, and creeks of Nova
Scotia, Magdalen Islands, and Labrador, so
long as the same shall remain unsettled ;
but so soon as the same, or either of
them, shall be settled, it shall not be lawful for the said fishermen to dry or cure
fish at such settlement without a previous
agreement for that purpose with the inhabitants, proprietors, or possessors of the
ground."

This provision conveyed to fishermen
from the United States two valuable privileges — that of fishing in British waters,
namely, within three miles of the British
coast, and that of drying and curing fish,
wherever caught, upon certain convenient
parts of the British coast. They had, of
course, like the men of all nations, apart

from any treaty stipulation, the right to fish outside the three mile limit, but this would avail them nothing, under the then mode of conducting the industry, unless they could freely make harbor in case of storm, and also land to cure their catch before lading it for the homeward cruise. What worth these rights had will be clear if we remember that fishing had always been one of New England's foremost trades, and that the waters off Newfoundland and Nova Scotia had from, and probably before, Columbus's time been known as the richest fishing grounds of the globe.

The commissioners at Ghent, who drew up the treaty ending the War of 1812, wrangled long over the question whether or not the war had nullified the just cited Article 3 of 1783. Unable to agree, they signed their treaty without deciding the question, leaving this for the future to settle as it might. Great Britain held that our former rights had lapsed by the war, and excluded our fishing vessels from the bays, harbors, and creeks named above.

Several of our vessels were arrested on charge of trespass. The utmost tension still existed, in spite of the peace, especially as in the United States the view prevailed that our rights by the old treaty had outlived the war, notwithstanding the silence of the Ghent document.

At length, in 1818, a new treaty was entered into upon the question, signed October 20th, ratified by England November 2d, and by the United States January 28, 1819. This instrument ignored our contention that Article 3 of the treaty of 1783 was of perpetual obligation, and restricted our right to fish in shore to the southern shores of the Magdalen Islands, the west and southwest coasts of Newfoundland from the Rameau Islands round to Quirpon Island, and the Labrador coast from Mount Joly northward. Only here could our fishermen fish within the three mile limit, and they could dry and cure only on the named parts of Labrador and Newfoundland, Magdalen Islands being now excluded from this use. Even on

Labrador and Newfoundland the privilege of drying and curing was to be cut off by settlement, except as agreement should be made beforehand with the inhabitants.

But the fateful clause of this treaty was the following: "And the United States hereby renounce forever any liberty heretofore enjoyed or claimed by the inhabitants thereof, to take, dry, or cure fish on or within three marine miles of any of the coasts, bays, creeks, or harbors of his Britannic Majesty's dominions in America not included within the above-mentioned limits: Provided, however, that the American fishermen shall be admitted to enter such bays or harbors for the purpose of shelter and of repairing damages therein, of purchasing wood, and of obtaining water, *and for no other purposes whatever.* But they shall be under such restrictions as may be necessary to prevent their taking, drying, or curing fish therein, or in any other manner whatever abusing the privileges hereby reserved to them."

Troubles were soon as abundant as ever.

The Canadians applied the word "bay" to all indentations of their coast, affecting entirely to exclude our fishermen from great bodies of water like Fundy, Chaleurs, and Miramichi, however far parts of these might be from shore. This was the famous "headland theory" for defining national waters. They also denied our right to navigate the Gut of Canso, which separates Cape Breton Island from Nova Scotia, thus forcing far out of their nearest course our ships bound for the permitted inshore fisheries. United States fishermen on their part persisted in exploiting the great bays, landed upon the Magdalen Islands, pushed through the Gut, and were none too careful at any point to find or heed the three mile line.

June 5, 1854, was signed a treaty of reciprocity between the United States and the British provinces, under which all the coasts of British North America were opened to our fishing vessels, in return for similar liberty to those of the provinces in all United States waters north of Cape May, latitude 36°, the salmon and

shad fisheries of each country being, however, reserved to itself. This arrangement
was to continue ten years at least, and then
to be terminable on a year's notice by
either of the high contracting parties.
Such notice having been given by the
United States one year before, reciprocity
in fishing privilege came to an end March
7, 1865. This, of course, renewed the wry
and perplexing rules of the 1818 convention, with all the naturally consequent
strife. The worst evils were, indeed, put
off for a time, by a continuance to our
vessels of the right to fish in provincial
water on the payment of a small license
fee. This favor was taken away in 1870,
for the alleged reason that American
captains failed to procure licenses, and in
the course of this year many of our ships
were seized and confiscated. New stern-
ness had been imparted to the provincial
policy by the Canadian Act of Confed-
eration, valid from July 1, 1867, which
joined Ontario and Quebec with Nova
Scotia and New Brunswick, thus inspiring

our neighbors to the north with a new sense of their strength and importance.

Now came the Treaty of Washington, 1871. Its Article 18 revived Article 1 of the 1854 Reciprocity Treaty, except that Canadians could now go so far south as the 39th parallel, and that two years' notice must precede abrogation. Article 21 ordained between the two countries free trade in fish-oil and in all salt-water fish. Both sides assumed that mere reciprocity would advantage the United States the more, so that by Article 22 a commission was provided for to award Canada a proper balance in money. By bungling diplomacy on our part the real power in this commission was swayed by M. Maurice Delfosse, Belgian minister at Washington, a gentleman certain to favor Great Britain at our expense. As a consequence, we were forced to pay for reciprocity to the round note of $5,500,-000. The money was a trifle; but its exorbitant amount had the unhappy effect of prejudicing our people against the new arrangement. The result was that at the earliest possible moment, viz., July 1, 1883, our Government gave the notice necessary for its abrogation.   This followed on July 1, 1885, in the very midst of the fishing season.   A temporary diplomatic arrangement was effected, which continued to our fishermen for the remainder of 1885 the advantages of the recent treaty; but with the dawn of the new year, 1886, the old convention of 1818 came once more into operation.

So soon as the fishing season was opened the plan of the British Government was evident.   It was to deny the fishing vessels all facilities not guaranteed by the treaty of 1818—that is, fishing vessels of the United States would be permitted to enter Canadian ports for shelter, repairs, wood, and water, and "for no other purposes whatever;" also to compel all such vessels strictly to conform to both customs and port laws.   Circular letters of instruction, enjoining vigilance, were sent to all customs officers, and swift cruisers fitted out to look sharply after all fishing vessels from the

States. On the other hand our fishermen were not, as a whole, disposed to conform to the existing regulations. The Treaty of Washington had been abrogated at their request, and now many, probably most, of them were inclined to exercise all the liberty possible in the Canadian waters. Least of all were they willing to submit to the British interpretation of the treaty of 1818.

Complaints early reached Washington that the headland theory was being applied by the provincial customs officials to exclude our vessels from legitimate fishing places; but the Canadian Government denied that any such thing had been done by its authority, and evidently did not incline to push its old contention on this point. While the fishing schooner Marion Grimes, of Gloucester, Mass., was under detention at Shelburne, Nova Scotia, for an infraction of the customs rules, her captain having hoisted the United States flag, this was pulled down by order of the Canadian officer in temporary charge of her.   The flag was again hoisted and again forcibly lowered.   This act awakened great resentment in the United States, until it, too, was disavowed by the Governor-General in Council.   The Sarah H. Prior lost at sea a valuable net, which a Canadian schooner picked up and wished to return. This was forbidden, and being permitted to purchase no other seine, the ship came home with a broken voyage and in debt. Captain Tupper, of the Jeannie Seaverns, having entered the harbor of Liverpool, Nova Scotia, for shelter, was denied permission to go and see his relatives near by or to receive them aboard his vessel. The water-tank of the schooner Mollie Adams having burst, her captain sought to buy two or three barrels to hold water for his crew on their homeward voyage of five hundred miles.   His request was refused.

The same Mollie Adams found a Nova Scotia vessel in distress and rescued her crew.   Captain Jacobs, of the Mollie, cared for the men several days, and finally, as no assistance of any sort was proffered by the Canadians, sent them home at his own expense. His aid to them delayed his homeward journey, and he was also caught in a harbor from which his vessel could pass only during very high water, which caused further delay. Owing to these incidents his supply of provisions ran low, yet he was denied permission to purchase anything, and as a result his homeward tour was made on half rations or less. Many other aggravating circumstances were connected with this case.

In quite a number of instances American masters were refused water, the only excuse being that they had not conformed to all the port or customs regulations. There can be no doubt that many fishing captains were quite too lax in this, presuming on the power of their nation and remembering the liberties enjoyed under reciprocity, while too forgetful of the stern letter of the treaty which the Canadians were executing against them. It was plain on the other hand that however wrongly Canadian subalterns may at times have acted, both the Canadian and the British Government intended to keep within the letter of the law, while forcing us to fish off their coasts at as great a disadvantage as possible.

The real source of the difficulty was well characterized by Mr. Phelps, our Minister to England. " It is to be found in the irritation that has taken place among a portion of the Canadian people on account of the termination by the United States Government of the treaty of Washington on the 1st of July, 1885, whereby fish imported from Canada into the United States, which so long as that treaty remained in force was admitted free, is now liable to the import duty provided by the general revenue laws ; and the opinion appears to have gained ground in Canada that the United States may be driven, by harassing and annoying their fishermen, into the adoption of a new treaty, by which Canadian fish shall be admitted free."

In their efforts to carry out such a policy the treaty gave the Canadians a very great

advantage. As Mr. Secretary Bayard insisted, it certainly trangressed usual international comity when our ships were
refused needed pilots, or our hungry crews
were forbidden to purchase food in Canadian ports ; but our President and Senate
had, in 1818, agreed that such cruelty
should be legal. To ask for comity in the
matter was to ask for the voidance of the
treaty.

As little could we, agreeably to the
treaty, presume, by use of home permits
to "touch and trade," to turn a fishing
vessel at will into a merchant vessel, as
was often tried in order to evade the offensive restrictions, or demand the liberty of
freighting fish home overland in bond. It
would equally have amounted to a quashing
of the treaty, had the British and Canadians interpreted it by the easy canon of
Mr. Phelps : "The question is not what is
the technical effect of the words, but what
is the construction most consonant to the
dignity, the just interests, and the friendly
relations of the sovereign powers."

Interesting but also untenable was our Government's plea for freedom to purchase bait for deep-sea fishing. Of old, mackerel had been caught almost solely with hooks, by the "chumming" process. In 1850 the purse seine was introduced. Soon after 1870 its use became general, and entirely revolutionized the business of taking mackerel. Huge quantities of the fish could now be captured far out in the open sea, making fishing much more profitable near home, and greatly lessening the value to us of Canada's fishing-grounds. From these premises Mr. Bayard argued that the true intent of the 1818 agreement, which was to protect inshore fishing territory, would not be violated should we be allowed to buy bait in Canada. It was replied that the old treaty was meant to prevent our fishermen from making Canadian harbors in any way a base of operations.

"It was framed with the object of affording a complete and exclusive definition of the rights and liberties which the fishermen of the United States were thenceforward to

enjoy in following their vocation, so far
as those rights could be affected by facilities for access to the shores or waters of the
British Provinces, or for intercourse with
their people.   It is therefore no undue
expansion of the scope of that convention
to interpret strictly those of its provisions
by which such access is denied, except to
vessels requiring it for the purposes specifi-
cally described.   Such an undue expansion
would, upon the other hand, certainly take
place if, under cover of its provisions, or of
any agreements relating to general commercial intercourse which may have since been
made, permission were accorded to United
States fishermen to resort habitually to the
harbors of the Dominion, not for the sake
of seeking safety for their vessels or of
avoiding risk to human life, but in order
to use those harbors as a general base of
operations from which to prosecute and
organize with greater advantage to themselves the industry in which they are engaged.

"Mr. Bayard suggests that the possession by a fishing vessel of a permit to 'touch and trade,' should give her a right to enter Canadian ports for other than the purposes named in the treaty, or, in other words, should give her perfect immunity from its provisions. This would amount to a practical repeal of the treaty, because it would enable a United States collector of customs, by issuing a license, originally only intended for purposes of domestic customs regulation, to give exemption from the treaty to every United States fishing vessel. The observation that similar vessels under the British flag have the right to enter the ports of the United States for the purchase of supplies loses its force when it is remembered that the convention of 1818 contained no restriction on British vessels, and no renunciation of any privileges in regard to them."

For some weeks in the spring and summer of 1886, the fishery dispute greatly excited our country. Even threats of war with Canada were uttered in case its government should not recede from its aggra-

vating position, and careful estimates made
of the force we could throw across our
northern border in three days. In May,
1886, Congress placed in the President's
hands power to suspend commercial intercourse between the two countries. Later
in the year a bill was introduced in the
House cutting off all commercial relations
with Canada by land or water. The Senate advanced a more moderate proposition,
to limit the proposed arrest of traffic to
water commerce and to Canadian vessels,
also to leave its enforcement optional with
the President. This became law on March
3, 1887. Under this legislation the President, on being assured that fishing masters
or crews were treated in Canadian ports
any less favorably than masters or crews of
trading vessels from the most favored nations, could, "in his discretion, by proclamation to that effect, deny vessels, their
masters and crews, of the British dominions
of North America, any entrance into the
waters, ports, or places of or within the
United States."

The President, however, did not think best at once to use this fearful power, likely enough to lead to war. He preferred to make another attempt at a peaceful settlement, through a new treaty. This had constantly been the wish of the British Government. Accordingly, later in the year 1887, a joint commission, consisting of Secretary Bayard, President Angell, of Michigan University, Hon. William L. Putnam, of Maine, on the part of the United States, and of Rt. Hon. Joseph Chamberlain, Sir Charles Tupper, of Canada, and Sir Lionel West, the British minister, on the part of Great Britain, met at Washington. The commission toiled nearly all winter, and passed to the President the result of its deliberations on February 16, 1888.

The treaty which it drafted was necessarily a compromise. Canada thought the British commissioners had yielded too much ; many in the United States believed our commissioners to have done the same. The document, approved by the President, went to the Senate, where, after long de-

bate, it was refused ratification, August
21st.

The commission had agreed upon a *modus
vivendi*, to hold good, unless revoked by
the Governor-General and Council of Canada, till February, 1890, under which our
fishermen might obtain in Canadian ports,
on payment of a license, the privileges of
merchantmen. Many such licenses were
taken out during the season of 1888, showing the advantages which they conveyed.
Most of the fishing-masters, however, did
not seek licenses and were averse to the
new treaty, preferring the terms of 1818
to granting their rivals any further rights
in our markets. Fresh fish, including
frozen and slack-salted, was already free
in our ports, competing sharply with our
own catch. No one longer cared to fish
inside, or, except in emergencies, to provision at Canadian towns. Convenient as
would be the power to obtain bait near
the fishing-grounds and to trans-ship fish
home in bond, neither was indispensable.
Cod are still caught with trawls and baited

hooks. The best bait is squid, whose abundance upon the Banks is what causes the cod so to frequent them. The squid can be had freshest as well as cheapest from the peasantry of the Newfoundland and Nova Scotia coasts; but clams carried from home were found to do nearly as well. They would remain fresh better than squid, but got off the hooks more easily. Accordingly, few collisions occurred in 1888, and as the season of that year closed there was prospect that, even without a new convention, no necessity for American retaliation would arise.

This chapter shall close with a word touching the Alaska fisheries question, which, fortunately, had advanced a good step. In 1870 the United States leased the Pribylov, or Seal Islands off Alaska, to the Alaska Commercial Co. Pressed by this company, which naturally wished the completest possible monopoly of seal-fishing, our Government foolishly affected to treat the entire Behring Sea as a *mare clausum*, belonging to the United States.

Several British craft engaged in taking seals were seized by United States vessels considerably more than three miles from land. Great Britain of course protesting, a treaty, ratified in March, 1892, submitted to arbitration the question between the two governments. Seven arbitrators sat, two from the United States, Justice Harlan and Senator Morgan, and one each from Canada, Great Britain, Sweden, France, and Italy. This Board decided against the American contention, denying the right of the United States to assume the protection of seals or any property in them outside the ordinary three-mile limit. Happy provisions were, however, made for a joint police of Behring Sea by the two nations, for an open and a closed fishing season, and for the careful licensing of sealing vessels.

CHAPTER IV.

THE SOUTH

It cannot be denied that the radical method of reconstruction resorted to by Congress occasioned dreadful evils. Among other things it ignored the natural prejudices of the whites, many of whom were as loyal as any citizens in the land. The South, subjected to a second conquest after having laid down its arms, felt outraged and grew sullen. To most people in that section, as well as to very many at the North, this dictation by Congress to acknowledged States in time of peace seemed high-handed and guilty usurpation. Northern Congressmen incessantly called slavery barbarism, and yet combined to transmute to-day into electors and law-makers those who but yesterday had been slaves. Black legislatures inevitably abused their power, becoming the instruments of base carpet-bag leaders and rings in robbing white property-holders.

Nor could any except doctrinaires or the stupid have expected that the whites would long submit to such a *régime*. If the South

[From the Independent Monitor, Tuscaloosa, Alabama, September 1, 1868.]
A PROSPECTIVE SCENE IN THE CITY OF OAKS, 4TH OF MARCH, 1869.

"Hang, curs, hang! * * * * * *Their* complexion is perfect gallows. Stand fast, good
fate, to *their* hanging! * * * * * If they be not born to be hanged, our case is miserable."
    The above cut represents the fate in store for those great pests of Southern society—
the carpet-bagger and scalawag—if found in Dixie's land after the break of day on the
4th of March next.

A Facsimile put in Evidence before the Congressional Committee.

was to become again genuine part and parcel of this Union, it could not, nor would the North consent that it should, be permanently under bayonet rule ; and so soon as bayonets were gone, fair means or foul would speedily remove the sceptre from

colored hands.   Precisely this happened.
In State after State, the whites, without
the slightest formal change of constitution
or law, recovered their ancient ascendency.
Where their aims could not be realized by
persuasion or other mild means, resort was
had to merciless intimidation and violence.

The Ku-Klux Klan, a great secret society, was organized for this rough business,
numbering at first, among either its members or its abettors, citizens of the highest
respectability.   Its local lodges were called
"dens," its members "ghouls."   "Giants,"
"goblins," "titans," "furies," "dragons,"
and "hydras," were names of different
classes among its officers.   Usually the very
existence of a "den" in the vicinity was
sufficient to render every negro docile.   If
more was required, a half-dozen ghouls,
making their nocturnal rounds in their hideous masks and uniforms, frightened all but
the most hardy.   Any who showed fight
were whipped, maimed, or killed, treatment
which extended on occasion to their "carpet-bag" and "scalawag" friends—these

titles denoting respectively northern and southern men bold enough to take the negroes' side. The very violence of the order, which it at last turned against the old Southrons themselves, brought it into disrepute with its original instigators, who were not sorry when federal marshals, put up to it by President Grant, hunted den after den of the law-breakers to the death.

Yet, after all, one cannot see how the giant problem of resuscitating the South could, under the circumstances, have been solved more successfully. The plan proposed by President Johnson had sufficient trial to show that it must have led to ills worse than those actually experienced. A qualified colored suffrage would, as things then were, have been abused. It must be remembered that the war left in the South much less of white loyalty than it found, and Congress was certainly justified in insisting that the revived States should be placed on the most loyal basis possible.

Withal, considering the stupendous upheaval in southern society marked by the erection of bondmen into full citizens, dark days were few. Schools arose, partly from the application of a large fund left by Mr. George Peabody for that purpose, partly from the beneficence of the various religious denominations interested in the elevation of the blacks, and partly from provision by the southern States themselves. The ballot itself proved an educator, rough but thorough. The negro vote, now that it had become a fixed fact, was little by little courted by the jarring factions of whites, and hence protected. Political parties, particularly in state elections, more and more divided on other lines than that of color. The administration of President Cleveland taught the negro that even in National affairs he had nothing to fear from democratic dominance. And it was plainly to the freedman's infinite advantage, meanwhile, that he was fighting not to acquire status and rights, but for acquired status and rights guaranteed in the organic law of his State and the Nation.

Among the white people loyalty to the

old flag increased with the days. Of course none of them would ever confess regret at having drawn the sword, or cease to think of the lost cause with a sigh. At the same time a rational conviction settled down upon all its most thoughtful minds that in secession the South had been misguided. Universal was the admission that at least for the dominant race the death of slavery was a blessing. Northern people and intelligent immigrants from Europe thronged in. Coolly received at first, and in some cases maltreated if freely expressing opinions which traversed those prevalent in the section, in the end they were tolerated and even welcomed.

The multiplication of railways facilitated the acquaintance of southern with northern people far beyond what had been possible before the war. Travelling salesmen from the North penetrated the remotest hamlets at the South, inclined from every consideration to produce the most favorable impression possible. The selection of southerners for important national offices

by Presidents Grant, Hayes, Arthur, and
Cleveland, the election of the last-named, a
Democrat, as President in 1884 and 1892,
and the existence of a democratic majority
in the House of Representatives almost
constantly from 1874, all felicitously combined to beget in the people of the South a
conviction that they were really and truly
citizens of the Union again. The rise in
several southern States of a strong republican organization among the whites wrought
in the same direction. Nor must we over-
look as another cementing influence the
fraternizing of northern and southern soldiers in great reunions such as occurred at
Gettysburg, Richmond, and Chickamauga.

The South's material prosperity kept pace
with her political advance. It had always
been said that cotton was to be produced
only by slave labor. Nothing could have
been more false. The largest cotton crop
under slavery, that of 1860, reached 4,669,-
770 bales. In 1871, 1876, and 1877 each,
notwithstanding the economic chaos and
the infinite destruction of capital occasioned

by the war, those figures were almost equalled; in 1878 they were surpassed; in 1879 and 1880 each, over 5,000,000 bales were raised; in 1881, 1883, and 1886 each, over 6,000,000, the exact figure for the year last named being 6,550,215. In 1890, 7,472,-511 bales were produced.

This cotton exhibit was sufficiently gratifying, yet the post-bellum crops might have been far larger had not much energy at the South been happily diverted into manufacturing channels. This was one of the most hopeful features of the New South. Nearly every department of industry in this kind was now pushed there at many points. Nashville became a great manufacturing and commercial city. It boasted one of the largest foundries in the country, and several flourishing cotton factories. Chattanooga, Birmingham, and Anniston were all thrifty with iron and steel industries, which rivalled the most prosperous ones at the North; nor were there wanting those who predicted that the region of those cities, viz., Southern Tennessee with Northern Georgia and Alabama, was speedily to become the centre of iron and steel production for the world.

The lumber trade of Chattanooga, particularly in the white woods, was said to be second only to Chicago's. The city also had a tannery believed to be the largest in the world, and more than one fully appointed Bessemer steel manufactory. These steel works and the tannery employed colored operatives almost alone, many of these exceedingly skilful. Birmingham was entirely a creation of the days since the war, yet it had in 1890 more than 26,000 inhabitants against 3,000 in 1880, and enjoyed marvellous prosperity, hindered only by speculation in land. Much of the marble in the mountains of Tennessee, Alabama, and Georgia was finer than any elsewhere to be found in this country. The block of it which was forwarded from Alabama for the Washington monument, experts condemned for the purpose as certainly Italian, nor was it permitted a place in that structure till the Governor of the

State and the Members of Congress there-
from had certified upon honor, and the
quarry-masters made affidavit, that it came
out of the Alabama hills. Atlanta had risen
from the ashes in which the war left it, to
be a city of over 65,000 people, with every
manifestation of great industrial life and
progress.

Between 1870 and 1880. although the
population of Mobile decreased, that of
Charleston rose about $1\frac{1}{5}$ per cent., that of
Savannah about $5\frac{1}{4}$ per cent., that of New
Orleans about thirteen per cent., that of
Richmond about twenty-six per cent. Between 1880 and 1890 Mobile advanced about
$6\frac{1}{2}$ per cent., Charleston almost 10 per cent.,
Savannah over 40 per cent., New Orleans
over 12 per cent., and Richmond exactly 28
per cent.

It would be misleading to suppose the
progress in welfare indicated by these and
the foregoing statements to be true of every
district at the South. The merely agricultural regions were still far behind. Methods
of tilling the soil were the same as prevailed

forty years earlier, and it was not unlikely
that the colored people, who for the most
part had the immediate charge of this work,
prosecuted it, as yet, with less skill than did
overseers and planters before slavery was
done away.   Yet in 1890 the farm valuation
of the South was found to exceed its highest
ante-bellum figure and almost to equal one-
fifth of the entire farm valuation of the
country.

To the general backwardness of southern
agriculture there was one quite striking
exception.   The State of Florida under-
went after the war a most astounding tran-
sition for the better.   Her total railway
mileage of 416 miles when the war ended
had grown to 2,470 miles by 1890.   The
farm valuation was, in 1880, $20,500,000.
The population in 1890 exceeded that
of 1880 by almost 50 per cent.   Steam-
boats were upon every coast and river.
This was due not alone to the State's
popularity as a winter sanitarium for
northern people.   Florida was also the
early market-garden for the North.   Its

oranges largely supplied the trade, and were much sought for their excellent quality. The State was excessively rich in the finest ornamental woods, which were rapidly finding their way into the market. Nearly

The Mouth of the Miami River, Florida.

all the crops of the temperate zone and the fruits of the torrid flourished here with the utmost luxuriance, many of them being natives, others taking to the soil with a greater friendliness than they displayed for that whence they were transplanted. The State bade fair to rival Louisiana in the production of sugar, and South Carolina in that of rice, as well as one day to supply the entire American demand for cocoanuts. The mulberry was indigenous to every part of this new Eden, which promised to become at no late date an immense producer of raw silk. Cattle fed and fattened everywhere without shelter, in winter as in summer.

The future of the colored race no one could predict with certainty. After the census of 1870, which reduced the percentage of our African population from 14.13, the figure in 1860, to 12.7, many rushed to the conclusion that these people might, in no long time, vanish from our land. The census of 1880 dispelled this fancy, raising the percentage to 13.12. That of 1890 lowered it again to 11.93. Previously to 1870 the race had been constantly decreasing in fecundity, but it was possible that the better conditions afforded by freedom had changed this. Even should the decrease go on, the colored people bade fair to be at least eight

or ten per cent. of our total population
in 1900. As a matter of fact the proportion was in 1900 11.6 per cent. These
decreasing proportions did not, of course,
necessarily imply any positive decadence
in the black race, as they might be ac-
counted for by greater prolificacy or vitality
on the part of the whites, or in part by immigration. The subject will be resumed
in Chapter IX. of Period VI.

CHAPTER V.

THE WEST

ASIDE from West Virginia, made during the war from the loyal part of Virginia, the new States created between 1860 and 1900 were Kansas, 1861; Nevada, 1864; Nebraska, 1867; Colorado, 1876; North Dakota, 1889; South Dakota, 1889; Montana, 1889; Washington, 1889; Idaho, 1890; Wyoming, 1890; and Utah, 1896. The whole number of States had thus become forty-five. We had also, in the year 1896, three organized territories, Arizona, New Mexico, and Oklahoma, the last carved out of Indian Territory in the year 1890. Alaska was as yet a partially organized territory, having no territorial legislature, and being under the laws of the United States and of the State of Oregon. It was purchased by the United States from Russia in 1867, for the sum of

$7,200,000.   It remained without any organ-
ization until the act of May 17, 1884, which
gave it a governor, a district court, an
attorney, a marshal, and commissioners.

The value to our Union of this new

The Site of Chicago.

acquisition, with its 531,409 square miles
and a coast-line longer than that upon our
Atlantic and Gulf coasts together, was at
first doubtful, and continued so till gold
was found on the Yukon and at Cape
Nome.   Clearly, however, the money
had not been thrown away.   Governor

Swineford, appointed over the Territory in
1885, declared that throughout Southern
Alaska and the Aleutian Islands the climate
was moderate, even in winter; and he gave
records of thermometrical observations
which seemed to prove this. He further
maintained that, in the parts named, all our
hardier plants and crops grew to maturity in summer, and attained extraordinary
luxuriance. In 1890, 4,298 white people
had homes in Alaska, besides 1,823 mixed,
23,531 Indians, and 2,288 Mongolians, a
total population of 32,052.

The Alaska Commercial Company paid
the United States $55,000 yearly for its
monopoly of the Alaska seal-fur trade. The
product of this business was about $2,500,-
000 each year. An official report made to
our Government stated that in the year
1880, $2,181,832 worth of Alaska furs found
sale in London alone. Coal had been dis-
covered in various places. So had beautiful
white marble. Gold-bearing ledges were
numerous, and the only one of these yet
broached, that on Douglas Island, had cer-

tainly yielded well. The mill connected with it, working only the equivalent of two-thirds time, turned out during its first twelve months a little over $750,000 worth of gold bullion. For the year 1889, according to imperfect returns, the product from this remote patch of our national domain was as follows : Seal fisheries, $314,925, a falling off of over 80 per cent. in nine years ; other fisheries, $1,059,365, an increase of about 100 per cent. for the same period; 43,762 troy ounces of gold and 9,219 troy ounces of silver. In 1890 there were ten manufacturing establishments, whose product amounted to $58,440.

After 1860 there was a steady filling up of the Pacific coast, and an equally continual extension of population to the west on the east side of the Rockies. All Iowa was in cultivation, and all Minnesota but the extreme northwest corner. In fifteen years the rate of interest went down in Iowa from ten to seven or eight per cent., in Michigan from ten to six or seven per cent. Chicago, from being only a borrower of money, grew to be an immense lender for enterprises in the West. Settlement in Kansas, Nebraska, and Texas rolled westward with strength and rapidity. Some of the finest new towns

An Ohio River Flat-Boat.

in these States were well toward their far western border.

The construction of the five great Pacific railway lines, the Northern, the Union, the Santa Fé, the Southern, and the Great

Northern, with their various branches,
brought into valuable employ infinite
reaches of fertile land previously as good
as desert. Texas made most remarkable
advance both in square miles occupied and
in density of population, brought about
by great extension of railway mileage, and
of cattle, sheep, and wheat culture. Large
patches of the Dakotas, Montana, and Idaho
filled with settlers. Colorado became a
giant in production, the rush of population
thither in consequence of very extensive
and rich mineral discoveries having been
a stampede almost like that of 1849–50 to
California. Every hill was black with
miners. The growth of New Mexico, Arizona, and Nevada, considering their natural
wealth, was slow, owing in part to Indian
hostilities. New Mexico fell from rank 37
in 1870 to rank 43 in 1890. Tucson, Ariz.,
according to the best figures, fell between
1880 and 1887, from 10,000 to 7,500 inhabitants. In material things Utah pros-
pered greatly under the thrift, economy,
and hard work of the Mormons. Here

mining and speculation were less rigidly
pressed, and more energy devoted to
agricultural pursuits.

An Irrigated Orange Grove at Riverside, California.

In California, a smaller proportion than
formerly of all industry was now applied to
mining, a larger to agriculture and cattle-
raising. Southern California became the

competitor of Florida as a winter residence.
Oregon and Washington vied with Minnesota for the world-medal in wheat culture.
Over the infinite pasture lands at both feet
of the Rocky Mountains roamed herds of
bullocks destined to feed distant cities in
America and in Europe. It was foreseen
that many of these lands would in the course
of time be ploughed, and by the aid of irrigation turned into corn-fields, wheat-fields,
and market-gardens, a process which in New
Mexico had already gone far. Even the tract
inclosed by the parallels 31° and 45° and the
meridians 100° and 120°, which long seemed
destined for perpetual sterility, spite of the
many enterprises conceived, and the others,
like the scheme of the Colorado River Irrigation Company, initiated for redeeming it,
grew valuable when it was believed that
the National Government would undertake
to irrigate there. Crops in that region
grew bountifully under irrigation, and permanent water-supplies could easily be created. Natural woodland existed there only
near the few streams, and of the scanty trees

which grew scarcely a single variety of hard wood was found ; but the state and national afforestation of vast tracts bade fair to change this. The region comprised in the States and Territories named was not only the richest precious-metal field in America, but one of the very richest on the globe.

The picture we have presented is too glowing for the year 1893–94, during which great depression afflicted the whole West; but this was only temporary. Recovery was indicated by the success of the Trans-Mississippi Exposition at Omaha, in 1898. There were 2,600,000 admissions. The total cash receipts were $1,761,364, and the stockholders in the enterprise were paid dollar for dollar.

The city of San Francisco had 500 inhabitants in 1840, 34,776 in 1850, 56,802 in 1860, 149,473 in 1870, 233,959 in 1880, 298,-997 in 1890. This progress may be taken as in some sense an index to that of the West as a whole, far more so than the apparently spasmodic increase in some of California's smaller centres. Los Angeles mounted from a population of 5,728 in 1870, and of 11,183 in 1880, to one of 50,395 in 1890. Oakland had but 10,500 in 1870. Ten years later the figure was 34,555; and in 1890 it was 48,682. Stockton leaped from 10,287 in 1880 to 14,424 in 1890. In 1858 Denver was uninhabited. In 1870 it numbered 4,759 souls; in 1880, 35,629; in 1890, 106,713. Portland, Oregon, had in 1890 46,000 inhabitants; in 1900, 90,000. In the decade 1880–90 Wyoming grew from 20,789 to 60,705.

The growth and prosperity of this great western section of our country become apparent from an inspection of the following table, compiled from authentic sources:

STATES.	Population. 1870.	Population. 1890.	Property valuation. 1880.	Property valuation. 1890.	Value of Farms. 1880.	Value of Farms. 1890.	Railway mileage. Miles. 1885.	Railway mileage. Miles. 1890.	Number of periodicals. 1880.	Number of periodicals. 1890.	Gold product. Troy Oz. 1880.	Gold product. Troy Oz. 1889.	Silver product. Troy Oz. 1880.	Silver product. Troy Oz. 1889.
California	560,247	1,208,130	$1,348,000,000	$2,533,733,627	$262,051,282	$697,116,630	3,044	4,356	364	639	829,677	608,882	890,158	1,062,578
Colorado	39,864	412,198	240,000,000	1,145,712,267	25,109,223	85,035,180	2,884	4,176	90	298	130,608	187,681	12,800,120	18,575,551
Dakota, North }	14,181	182,719	118,000,000	337,006,506	22,401,084	75,310,805	2,677	2,003	66	139	159,920	149,533	54,770	104,672
Dakota, South }		328,808		425,141,299		107,466,335		2,470		269				
Idaho	14,999	84,335	29,000,000	207,896,591	2,882,890	17,431,580		944	8	58	71,578	95,983	359,309	3,137,508
Kansas	364,399	1,427,096	760,000,000	1,799,343,501	235,178,936	559,726,046	4,441	8,806	349	759				
Minnesota	439,706	1,301,826	792,000,000	1,691,851,927	198,724,260	340,059,470	4,381	5,879	224	553				
Montana	20,595	132,159	40,000,000	453,135,209	3,234,504	25,512,340	1,047	2,181	18	90	87,354	151,861	2,246,938	13,511,455
Nebraska	122,993	1,058,910	385,000,000	1,275,635,514	105,932,541	402,358,913	2,988	5,300	189	645				
Nevada	42,491	45,761	156,000,000	180,323,668	5,408,825	12,389,410	945	924	37	26	286,469	169,617	9,614,561	4,696,605
New Mexico	91,874	153,593	49,000,000	231,459,897	5,514,399	8,140,800	1,195	1,324	18	59	2,387	39,457	903,455	1,251,124
Oregon	90,923	313,767	154,000,000	590,396,194	56,908,575	115,819,200	1,181	1,433	74	194	53,101	46,648	21,496	17,851
Texas	818,579	2,235,523	825,000,000	2,105,576,766	170,468,886	399,971,289	6,687	8,630	279	678		330		323,438
Utah	86,736	207,905	114,000,000	349,411,234	14,015,178	25,402,720	1,085	1,085	24	71	14,105	23,591	3,668,566	7,005,198
Washington	23,955	349,390	62,000,000	760,698,726	13,844,224	83,461,660	736	1,774	29	253	6,569	9,005	789	28,464
Wyoming	9,118	60,705	54,000,000	169,773,710	835,595	14,460,980	617	941	10	43	888	711		
TERRITORIES.														
Alaska		32,052								4	288	43,762	39	9,219
Arizona	9,658	59,620	41,000,000	188,880,976	1,127,946	7,222,230	906	1,096	17	35	10,254	44,029	1,798,921	1,812,961

We shall be pardoned for recurring
again to Minnesota. So recently as 1838,
where St. Paul and Minneapolis now stand,
the former with a population in 1890 of

The Irrigating Reservoir at Walnut Grove, Arizona, showing the Artificial Lake
partly filled.

133,156, the latter with one of 164,738, not a
white man's abode had risen. There were
then but three cabins between St. Paul and
Prairie du Chien, a distance of 300 miles
down the Mississippi. Summit Avenue,

St. Paul, was, in 1890, the finest street in
America, if not on the globe.   West St.
Paul, in 1880 a hamlet of a few huts, had
by 1890 20,000 to 30,000 people, with
street-cars, large business blocks, fine
houses and stores.   The pioneer railway in
Minnesota was laid in 1862, from St. Paul
to St. Anthony, the first shovelful of earth
being lifted by a citizen of St. Paul, who
probably lived to see his State gridironed
with 5,379 miles of track, his own firm constructing over 1,100 miles in the single
year 1887.   Minneapolis in 1887 turned
out 5,000,000 barrels of flour, an average
of 100,000 barrels a week.

Duluth had in 1880 but 3,740 people.   In
1890, 33,115.   The cause of Duluth's advantage is obvious upon a glance at the
map.   It is by water no farther from Lake
Erie than Chicago is, while it is some hundreds of miles nearer the great wheat-field.
It is itself the very gate of this—the gate
of Minnesota—which in 1869 brought forth
18,000,000 bushels ; in 1886, 50,000,000
bushels.   To this enormous yield, that

of the Dakotas, about the same, had now to be added, the one as the other finding its way out to the hungry world largely through Duluth.

The caravans of people necessary to populate these immense western ranges were to a very great extent immigrants from Europe. The census of 1880 gave us 6,679,043 inhabitants of foreign nativity. We have no figures for the exact proportion of the total immigration into the country which found its home in the West, yet a glimpse at the total from year to year is interesting at this point. The falling off in and after 1893 is particularly noticeable. Immigrants arrived as follows :

In 1868..........282,189	In 1880..........457,257
" 1869..........352,768	" 1881..........669,431
" 1870..........387,203	" 1882..........788,992
" 1871.......... 321,350	" 1883..........603,322
" 1872..........404,806	" 1884..........518,592
" 1873..........459,803	" 1885..........395,346
" 1874..........313,339	" 1886..........334,203
" 1875..........227,498	" 1890..........455,302
" 1876..........169,986	" 1891..........560,319
" 1877..........141,857	" 1892..........579,663
" 1878..........138,469	" 1893..........439,730
" 1879..........177,826	" 1894..........285,631

CHAPTER VI.

IT was fitting that the one hundredth anniversary of a great industrial nation should be celebrated by a World's Fair. Such a plan was first publicly proposed for the United States in 1870, by an association of Philadelphia citizens. It was adopted by Congress in the following year, when an act was passed creating a Centennial Commission, to consist of a delegate and an alternate from each State and Territory. The commission organized for the great and difficult work before them by choosing General J. R. Hawley, of Connecticut, president, and by appointing an executive committee, a board of directors, and heads of various administrative bureaus.

The Government declined to assume the

financial responsibility of the enterprise,
but in 1872 Congress appointed a Centennial Board of Finance with power to raise
a capital stock of $10,000,000. Shares to
the amount of $2,400,000 were soon sold to

At the Centennial Exposition, Philadelphia, 1876.

private citizens. Philadelphia appropriated
$1,500,000, and Pennsylvania $1,000,000.
In 1876 Congress made a loan to the
Board of $1,500,000. Thus the great
problem of a financial basis for the enterprise was solved.

The first thought had been to make the

exposition exclusively national, but subsequent deliberation made it seem best to widen the plan so that the arts and industries of the entire world should be represented.   President Grant formally proclaimed the Exhibition in 1873, and in the following year foreign governments were invited to participate.   Thirty-three cordially responded.

Meanwhile, the commission was pushing preparations.   Philadelphia, the birth-place of the nation, was rightly chosen as the place for this unique memorial of that event.   In the beautiful and spacious Fairmount Park, on the high bank of the Schuylkill River, an area of 285 acres was inclosed, and here five main buildings were soon rising rapidly as by magic.   Besides these, there were at the time of opening, smaller structures to the number of 175, filling every available space.

On May 10th the Exposition was opened with appropriate exercises, in the presence of 100,000 people.   Wagner had composed a Centennial March for the occasion.   Whit-

tier's Centennial Hymn was sung by a
chorus of 1,000 voices. The restored South
chanted the praises of the Union in the
words of Sidney Lanier, the Georgia poet.
President Grant, in a short speech, then declared the International Exhibition open.
A procession of dignitaries moved to Machinery Hall, where the President of the
United States and Dom Pedro II., Emperor
of Brazil, set in motion the great Corliss
engine, and with the whirr of spindle and
clatter of machinery the world's seventh
great fair began.

Weeks and months of inspection were
necessary to grasp the Exhibition as a
whole and in detail, but an imaginary stroll
through the grounds will give the reader
some general idea of it.

Entering through one of the 106 gates,
the sight-seer naturally turned his eye first
toward the colossal Main Building. A
parallelogram in form, 1,880 feet long by
460 wide, and 70 high, it covered twenty
acres. At the centre and ends were projecting wings, large buildings in themselves.

In the middle and at the four corners rose
towers.   In spite of its size the building
seemed light and almost graceful. Its brick
sub-structure, seven feet high, stood upon
massive masonry foundations.   The rest of
the building was mainly glass and iron.
The iron trusses of the roof rested upon
672 slender iron pillars.   This hall had
been erected in a year, at a cost of
$1,700,000.

In the Main Building manufactures were
exhibited, also products of the mine, along
with various other evidences of the condition of science and education.   The broad
aisles ran the whole length of the interior,
flanked on either side by exhibits.   More
than one-third of the space was reserved
for the United States, the rest being divided in varying proportions among foreign
countries.   The products of all climates,
tribes, and times were here crowded together under one roof.   The mighty states
of Great Britain, France, and Germany
exhibited the work of their myriad roaring
looms side by side with the wares of the

Hawaiian Islands and the little Orange
Free State. Here were the furs of Russia
with other articles from the frozen North;
there the flashing diamonds of Brazil and
the rich shawls and waving plumes of India.
At a step one passed from old Egypt to
the latest-born South American republic.
Chinese conservatism and Yankee enterprise confronted each other across the aisle.
All civilized nations but Greece were represented—more than ever before took part
in an international fair.

From the novelty of the foreign display
the American visitor returned proudly to
the display made by his own land. Textiles,
metal work, arms and tools, musical instruments, watches, carriages, cutlery, books,
and furniture—a bewildering array of all
things useful and ornamental—made Americans realize as never before the wealth,
intelligence, and enterprise of their native
country and the proud station she had
taken among the nations of earth.

Machinery Hall came next to the Main
Building in size. Of plain architecture,

built of wood, with iron ties, 1,402 feet by 360, it covered, with an annex, about thirteen acres. Here, with infinite clatter and roar, thousands of iron slaves worked their master's will. Three-fourths of the space was taken up with American machines. Visitors from the foremost foreign nations marvelled at the ingenuity of the Yankee mind here displayed. Great Britain led the foreign nations in the size and number of articles exhibited. Canada, France, Russia, Sweden, Brazil, and other countries sent ingenious or powerful machines.

But as a Titan, towering above all these and all others, stood the great Corliss engine, built by George H. Corliss, of Providence, R. I., one of the most remarkable mechanicians and inventors of the century. A modern Samson, dumb as well as blind, its massive limbs of shining steel moved with voiceless grace and utmost apparent ease, driving the miles of shafting and the thousands of connected machines. The cylinders were forty inches in diameter ; the piston stroke, ten feet. The great walking-beams, nine feet wide in the centre, weighed eleven tons each. The massive fly-wheel, thirty feet in diameter, and weighing fifty-six tons, made thirty-six revolutions a minute. The whole engine, with the strength of 1,400 horses, weighed 700 tons.

Agricultural Hall, built of wood and glass in the form of a nave with three transepts, covered ten acres. The display it contained of agricultural products and implements was the largest ever made. Here the United States stood forth far in advance of all sister nations. Specimens of the rich and deep prairie soil excited the wonder and envy of tillers of impoverished European lands. The great West, with its monster steam-ploughs and threshing machines, placed before the eye the farming methods of a race of giants. The choice and delicate fruits of sunny lands mingled with the hardy cereals of Canada and Russia.

Memorial Hall, a beautiful permanent building of granite, erected by Pennsylvania and Philadelphia at a cost of $1,500,000, was given up to art. This was on the whole the poorest feature of the Exposition. America had few works of the first order to show. Foreign nations, with the exception of England, feared to send their choicest art products across the ocean. France, Germany, Spain, Belgium, and the Netherlands, with some other countries, were all represented. Italy, besides paintings, sent many pieces of sculpture. England contributed a noble lot of paintings, including works by Gainsborough and Reynolds. In spite of all, the collection was the largest and most notable ever seen in this country, and throngs crowded the galleries.

Horticultural Hall, built of iron and glass in the Moorish style of the twelfth century, also a permanent structure, was erected by Philadelphia. Here, one walked amid the glories of tropical vegetation. Palm, orange, lemon, camphor, and india-rubber trees rose on every hand. The cactus of the desert, rare English flowering plants, strange growths from islands of the sea, here flourished each in its peculiar soil and climate. Outside the building were beds of hardy flowering plants covering twenty-five acres. Besides these five main structures, the United States Building, where the working of the various administrative departments of the Government was shown, attracted thousands of visitors daily. A Woman's Pavilion contained products of female industry and skill. A narrow-gauge railway ran in great loops from building to building.

Twenty-six States erected buildings of their own. These served mainly as headquarters, but two or three contained large exhibits of state products. Thirty or more buildings were put up by private enterprise to illustrate various manufacturing and industrial processes. Before the close of the Exposition more than two hundred buildings stood within the enclosure. Several foreign Governments erected small structures of various sorts.

Through the summer months, in spite of the unusual heat that season, thousands of pilgrims from all parts of the country found their way to this shrine of the world's progress. The quiet old Quaker city was moved with unwonted life. Amidst the crowds of new-comers its citizens became strangers in their own streets.

On July 4th, simple but impressive ceremonies were held in the public square at the rear of Independence Hall. On temporary platforms sat 5,000 distinguished guests, and a chorus of 1,200 singers. The square and the neighboring streets were filled with a dense throng. Richard Henry Lee, grandson of the mover of the Declaration of Independence, came to the front with the original document in his hands. At sight of that yellow and wrinkled paper, the vast audience burst forth into prolonged cheering. Mr. Lee then read the Declaration. The recitation of an ode by Bayard Taylor and the delivery of an oration by Hon. William M. Evarts were the other main features of the exercises.

Through the early fall the interest in the Exposition spread farther and farther over the land, and the attendance steadily increased. On September 28th, Pennsylvania day, 275,000 persons passed through the gates. During October, the visitors numbered over 2,500,000. From May 10th to November 10th, the total admissions were 9,900,000 ; 8,000,000 admission fees were collected, amounting to $3,800,000. The fair was brought to an end on November 10th. After brief closing exercises, President Grant gave the signal to stop the Corliss engine. The giant slowly came to a standstill, the hum of the machinery died away, and the International Exhibition of 1876 was closed.

The Centennial Exposition was not a complete financial success. After returning the United States loan of $1,500,000, the stockholders could not be paid in full. The attendance was, however, larger in the aggregate than at any previous international exhibition, except that of Paris in 1867. The admissions there reached 10,200,000, but the gates were open fifty-one days longer than at Philadelphia. At Vienna, in 1873, there were but 7,255,000 admissions in 186 days against 159 days at Philadelphia.

The larger and more important results of this exposition cannot be measured with precision. A thousand silent influences were set at work upon our social, intellectual, and political life, which operated in secret for years afterward. The most obvious, and perhaps the most important, effect was the broadening of sympathies and mental outlook. Visitors to Philadelphia got something of the benefit of foreign travel. Local prejudices were broken down. New ideas of life and civilization were planted in hitherto sterile minds. The plodding Eastern farmer caught something of the Westerner's dash and swing. North and South, East and West, drew nearer together. A narrow patriotism caught glimpses of a great and noble world without.

These influences touched the most careless observer. Special classes derived each a peculiar benefit. Mechanical invention was stimulated. Art received an impetus which can never cease to be felt. To our household art, especially, came much quick-

ening from the sight of England's beautiful
display of home decorations.

The Exposition exalted the United States
in the eyes of her foreign guests. Many
were amazed at such proofs of the wealth,
intelligence, and progressive spirit of the
great republic. A correspondent of the
London *Times* wrote, in 1876 : " The
American invents as the Greek sculptured
and the Italian painted ; it is genius." We
may hope that the exhibits were educators
to Europe as well as to America.

Lastly, the American returned from the
great fair with an opinion of his own country which, if more sober and just than he
had previously entertained, was not less
proud but far prouder. The Nation laid
aside its holiday attire, and, despite mani-
fest defects and dangers in our national life,
settled down to another century of work
with increased pride in its past and stronger
confidence for its future.

CHAPTER VII.

ECONOMIC POLITICS

THE enormous strides with which we paid off our war debt amazed the world. The debt had reached its highest point in August, 1865. At that date the figure was $2,844,649,626, or, for the interest-bearing part alone, $2,381,530,294. The total interest-bearing debt on April 30, 1888, was only $1,038,199,762. At the end of that fiscal year, June 30, 1888, the debt, less cash in the treasury, amounted to $1,165,584,656. Its items at this time were $222,207,050 in bonds at 4½ per cent., payable in 1891; $714,315,450 in four per cent. bonds, payable in 1907; four per cent. refunding certificates amounting to $141,300; the three per cent. navy pension fund of $14,000,000, and the Pacific Railway six per cent. bonds, $64,623,512. Thus on June 30, 1888, more than half of the largest total had been paid off, and the net debt, aside from the Pacific Railway bonds, which that corporation was to pay, having fallen to below a billion. The reduction proceeded for the entire twenty-three years between the first and last dates named, at an average rate of $62,906,975 yearly, or $5,225,581 each month, $174,186 each day, $7,258 each hour, and $120.47 each minute.

The interest-bearing legal tender notes were first paid off. Greenbacks, or non-interest-bearing legal tenders were still, October 1, 1894, outstanding to the amount of $346,681,000; yet this division of the debt, too, had been vastly reduced, having stood at $433,160,569 on August 31, 1865.

To the bonded obligations of the country the policy of refunding was early applied, bonds of high rates being called in so soon as callable, and replaced by others bearing lower rates. The income of the Government was so immense that it proved unfortunate to have set so late a date as 1891 for the time at which the 4½'s could be

paid off. To fix the date of maturity for
the 4's in 1907 was, of course, worse still.
The three per cents. of 1882, which sup-
planted earlier issues, were fortunately made
payable at the Government's option, and
on May 20, 1887, the Secretary of the
Treasury issued a call for the last of· them,
amounting to $19,717,500, interest to cease
with the first of the next July.

From this time there were no bonds subject to par payment at the discretion of the
Government, and as revenues were vast the
surplus began to pile up in the treasury.
December 1, 1887, after every possible obligation of the Government had been provided for, $55,258,701 remained, a sum in-
creased by the end of that fiscal year,
namely, June 30, 1888, spite of considerable
amounts in long bonds purchased at high
rates, to $103,220,464. There was no
method at once legal and economical for
paying this out. The Secretary could of
course buy 4's and 4½'s in the open market,
and during 1888 this was to some extent
done. Obviously, if entered upon in a

large way, it must have greatly carried up the price of those bonds. The question how to limit the surplus, how to keep the money of the country from becoming locked up in the treasury and sub-treasuries of the United States, was thus a grave one, and entered hotly into the political campaign of the last-named year.

On June 30, 1890, $109,015,750 in the 4½ per cent. bonds, redeemable September 1, 1891, were still outstanding. By April 1, 1891, they had, by redemption or purchase, been reduced to $53,854,250, of which one-half in value was held by national banks, to sustain their circulation. To avoid contracting this circulation the Secretary of the Treasury permitted holders of these bonds to retain them and receive interest at two per cent. About $25,364,500 was so continued. Interest on the remainder ceased at their maturity, and nearly all were soon paid off. The bonds continued at two per cent. were all along quoted at par, though payable at the will of the Government, revealing a national credit never excelled in history. The national debt, less cash in the treasury, stood on July 1, 1894, after an increase during the previous fiscal year of $60,000,-000, at $899,313,381.

The old tariff issue had emerged again soon after the end of the war. The Morrill tariff of 1861 about restored the rates of 1846, and even those rates had, on many things, been very decidedly increased during the war. Still further protective duties had been laid in the course of the war, called compensating duties, to offset the internal revenues which burdened manufacturers in various ways. After the war the internal taxes were nearly all swept away at the earliest possible moment, until, after July 1, 1883, only spirits, fermented liquors, tobacco, banks and bankers yielded internal revenue. Customs duties were also removed from nearly all so-called revenue articles, as spices, tea, and coffee, not produced in this country—the tax, therefore, not being of a protective nature. Slight reductions were, indeed, made in

protective duties, first in 1872 — replaced,
however, almost entirely in 1875 — and
again in 1883. The act of 1883 lowered
protection less than appeared, and its rates
on woollens, high grade cottons, iron ore,
steel, and a few other articles, were now
made even higher than the same had previously borne. It will be seen that our
policy during the years under survey was
to limit national income sufficiently without lowering or removing any protective
duties.

In the republican platform of 1888 this
policy was explicitly avowed. At that time,
as next to nothing could at present be
done to pay off the national indebtedness,
both parties had to admit that some measure was needed to lessen the revenue. The
republican plan was to effect the reduction
mainly by lowering or removing the remaining internal taxes, the democratic to
secure the same result by changes in customs duties, cutting down rates and enlarging the free list. President Cleveland's
message to Congress in December, 1887,

stated the issue with great clearness, and this issue was the main one which divided the two parties in the presidential election of the ensuing year.

Anticipating a little we may remark in this place that the Republicans, having acquired control of all three legislative branches of the Government, passed, in 1890, the McKinley Tariff Act, considerably raising rates, though somewhat enlarging the free list. It removed the duty from raw sugar, affixing a bounty to the production of sugar in the United States. But in 1892 the Democrats again acquired power, electing Mr. Cleveland and controlling the Senate. In 1894 they passed the Wilson-Senate Tariff Act, greatly reducing rates in general, and free-listing the important commodities of wool, salt, and lumber. Raw sugar was now taxed again, and the bounty upon its production abolished.

The revenue question in this campaign was not a little complicated by the existence of numerous and powerful Trusts, which anti-protectionists believed to be fostered by our high tariff. The Trust System arose about 1876, and in the course of a few years almost every great enterprise in the land was carried on under the form of a trust. The principal corporations or men engaged in an industry would enter into combination, more or less informal, for the regulation of production and prices. Usually the result was an elevation of prices, and where the trust constituted a necessary monopoly this rise might be indefinitely perpetuated. High tariff as well as low tariff newspapers made great outcry against these monopolies. The latter urged that a reduced tariff, forcing these businesses more into competition with corresponding producers abroad, was the only thing needful to break their solidarity and consequent power. Advocates of high tariff denied this.

The old silver dollar, "the Dollar of the Fathers," had, until 1873, never ceased to be full legal tender, although it had since 1853 been too valuable as compared with the gold dollar to circulate much. In

1873 a law was passed demonetizing it, and making gold the exclusive form of United States hard money. The new German Empire did the same this very year. There at once began a great apparent depreciation of silver in comparison with gold at the historic ratio. For a long time this change involved no decrease in the value or purchasing power of silver even in the form of bullion, but consisted rather in a rise of the value of gold.

In view of this, as all the Government bonds outstanding in 1873 had been made payable in coin, it was as good as universally believed in most sections of the Union that the demonetizing of silver, if persisted in, would work hardship to taxpayers in liquidating the national debt. A bill was therefore brought forward, and in 1878 passed, restoring to the silver dollar its full legal tender character. In this legislation, however, so great was the then disparity in value between gold and silver at the ratio of 16 to 1, Congress did not venture to give back to the white metal

the right of free coinage, but instead required the Secretary of the Treasury to
purchase monthly not less than $2,000,000
worth of silver and coin it into dollars.

The act was disapproved by President
Hayes, but immediately passed over his
veto, February 28, 1878. The advocates of
gold monometallism believed that the issue
of these dollars would speedily drive gold
from the country. Owing to the limitation
of the new coinage no such effect was experienced, and the silver dollars, or the certificates representing them, floated at par
with gold, which, indeed, far from leaving
the country, was imported in vast amounts
nearly every year. After 1880 the money
in circulation in the United States was gold
coin, silver coin gold certificates, greenbacks or United States notes, and the notes
of the national banks. The so-called Sherman Law, of 1890, added a new category,
the treasury notes issued in payment for
silver bullion. It stopped the compulsory
coinage of full-tender silver, though con-
tinuing and much increasing the purchase

of silver bullion by the Government. The repeal of the purchase clause of this law, in 1893, put an end to the acquisition of silver by the United States.

January 1, 1879, the next year after the silver bill was passed, the United States, under the Resumption Act of January 14, 1875, began again the payment, which had been suspended ever since 1862, of specie in liquidation of greenbacks. The possibility of this had been under discussion for some years, and was disbelieved in by many thoughtful financiers and public men. The credit of the momentous step was mostly due to John Sherman, Secretary of the Treasury in the cabinet of President Hayes. He believed resumption to be as possible as it was important. By the sale of 4½ per cent. bonds redeemable in 1891, he had accumulated before the appointed day $138,000,000 of coin, nearly all in gold, amounting to about forty per cent. of the greenbacks then outstanding.

Resumption proved easier than even he anticipated. The greenbacks had risen to par—the first time in seventeen years—December 18th, thirteen days before the date fixed for beginning gold payments, and when the day arrived only straggling applications for coin were made, less in amount than was asked for in greenbacks as interest by bondholders, who could have demanded coin.   During the entire year only $11,-456,536 in greenbacks were offered for redemption, while over $250,000,000 in them were paid out in coin obligations.   It was found that people preferred paper to metal money, and had no wish for gold instead of notes when assured that the exchange could be made at their option.   Notwithstanding our acceptance of greenbacks for customs—$109,467,456 during 1879—the treasury at the end of that year experienced a dearth of these and a plethora of coin, having actually to force debtors to receive hard money.

Such popularity of the greenbacks stimulated to fresh life the " fiat greenback " theory, long in vogue and very influential in many parts of the country.   Its pith lay in the proposition that money requires in its material no intrinsic value, its worth and purchasing power coming entirely from the " fiat " of the government issuing it, so that paper money put forth by authority of a solvent and powerful government will be the peer of gold.   This idea was the rallying point of the National Labor Greenback Party, organized at its Indianapolis convention, May 17, 1876, when Peter Cooper was put in nomination for President.   At the subsequent presidential election in November, he received 82,640 votes.   The next year his party polled 187,095 votes ; in 1878, 1,000,365.

From the moment of its issue, there had been in the country many who went to the opposite extreme with reference to the greenback.   They believed it unconstitutional and pernicious, a menace to the nation's credit and financial weal.   The question came to the Supreme Court during the war, and this form of contracting debt on the part of the Government was then justified as a war measure.   When the war was over the question whether the greenback's legal tender quality could still be maintained, also had to be passed upon by the court. The first decision was in the negative, but it was subsequently reversed. Still a third question was whether a man could be forced to take greenbacks in liquidation of debt after the resumption of specie payments. This was tried out in the famous case of Juilliard *vs.* Greenman, and the decision was, as on the other two occasions, in favor of the greenback. In spite of all this, however, the zeal for the fiat or non-promissory theory and practice of paper money almost totally died away after about 1880.

The most desperate and extensive strike that had yet occurred in this country was that of 1877, by the employees of the principal railway trunk lines, the Baltimore and Ohio, the Pennsylvania, the Erie, the New York Central, and their western prolongations. At a preconcerted time junctions and other main points were seized. Freight traffic on the roads named was entirely suspended, and the passenger and mail service greatly impeded. When new employees sought to work, militia and United States troops had to be called out to preserve order. Baltimore and Pittsburgh were each the scene of a bloody riot. At the latter place, where the mob was immense and most furious, the militia were overcome and besieged in a roundhouse, which it was then attempted to burn by lighting oil cars and pushing them against it. Fortunately the soldiers escaped across the river. The torch was applied freely and with dreadful effect. Machine-shops, warehouses, and 2,000 freight-cars were pillaged or burnt. The loss of property was estimated at $10,000,000. In disturbances at Chicago nineteen were killed, at Baltimore nine, at Reading thirteen, and thrice as many wounded. One hundred thousand laborers were believed to have taken part in the movement, and at one time or another 6,000 or 7,000 miles of road were in their power. The agitation began on July 14th and was serious till the 27th, but had mostly died away by the end of the month, the laborers nearly all returning to their work.

Hosts of Pennsylvania miners went out along with the railroad men. The railway strike itself was largely sympathetic, the ten per cent. reduction in wages assigned as its cause applying to comparatively few. The next decade witnessed continual troubles of this sort, though rarely if in any case so serious, between wage-workers and their employers in nearly all industries. The worst ones befell the manufacturing portions of the country. Strikes and lock-outs were part of the news almost every day. The causes were various. One lay in the vast numbers of immigrants hither and the low, ignorant character of many of them—clay for the hand of the first unscrupulous demagogue.

Another cause was the wide and sedulous inculcation in this country of the communist and anarchist doctrines long prevalent in Europe. Influences concurrent with both these were the actual injustice and the proud, overbearing manner of many employers. Capital had been mismanaged and wasted. The war had brought unearned fortunes to many, sudden wealth to a much larger number, while the unexampled prosperity of the country raised up in a perfectly normal manner a wealthy class, the like of which, in number and power, our country had never known before. As therefore immigration along with much else multiplied the poor, the eternal, angry strife of wealth with poverty, of high with low, of classes with masses, crossed over from Europe and began on our shores.

The rise of trusts and gigantic corporations was connected with this struggle. Corporations worth nigh half a billion dollars apiece were able to buy or defy legislatures and make or break laws as they pleased ; and as such corporations, instead of individuals, more and more became the employers of labor, not only did the old-time kindliness between help and hirers die out, but men the most cool and intelligent feared the new power as a menace to democ-

racy. Strikes therefore commanded large
public sympathy. Stock-watering and other
vicious practices, involving the ruin of corporations themselves by the few holders of
a majority of the shares, in order to re-pur-
chase the property for next to nothing, con-
tributed to this hostility; as did the presence
in many great corporations of foreign capital and capitalists, and also the mutual
favoritism of corporations, showing itself,
for instance, in special freight rates to privi-
leged concerns. Minor interests and individ-
ual employees, powerless against these
Titan agencies by any of the old legal
processes, resorted to counter organization.

The Patrons of Husbandry grew up in
the West, with influence longer than the
Order's nominal life, of which the often
unwise " Granger " railroad legislation was
one sign. In the East trades-unions secured
rank development, and the Knights of
Labor, intended as a sort of Union of them
all, attained in 1887 a membership of a
million. The manufacturers' " black list,"
to prevent any " agitator " laborer from

securing work, was answered by the "boy-
cott," to keep the products of obnoxious
establishments from finding sale. Labor
organizations, so strong, often tyrannized
over their own members, and boycotting
became a nuisance that had to be abated
by law.

Labor agitation had of late years become
greatly easier owing to the extraordinarily
increased percentage of our urban population. In 1790 only 3.3 per cent. of the
people in the country lived in places of
8,000 inhabitants and upward, and so
late as 1840 only 8.5 per cent. In
1850 the percentage was 12.5; in 1860,
16.1; in 1870, 20.9; in 1880, 22.5; and in
1890, 29.2. The year 1880 saw within our
borders twenty cities each with a population
of over 100,000; 286 each with over 8,000.
In 1890 there were twenty-eight cities each
having 100,000 inhabitants or more, and
448 having 8,000 or more. It was mostly
manufacturing and mechanical industry
which thus brought these hordes of human
beings together.

CHAPTER VIII.

THE MARCH OF INDUSTRY

WE can give but little idea of the advance in industrial artifice and appliances of all kinds made in the United States in the two decades after the Civil War. Take it first in textile manufacturing. A century earlier one person in every family had to work incessantly at spinning and weaving to keep the whole of them in clothing. Now one day's work a year per person sufficed for this. The speed of spindles had risen since 1860 from 5,000 to 7,500 revolutions a minute. Looms had gone from 120 picks to 160, and one hand tended from 25 to 50 per cent. more work. The "slasher" dresser accomplished ten times more than the old machine, supplying 400 looms in place of forty, and requiring to manage it only one man and a boy instead of two men

The American Line Steamship St. Louis, launched from the Cramps Docks, November 12, 1894.

(554 feet long, 11,000 tons, and 20,000 horse-power.)

and ten girls. A generation earlier one operative made three yards an hour, now he made ten. In the twenty years under survey the annual production of cotton mills rose from two and one-half to three and one-half tons per hand. One man formerly tended forty spindles, now he tended sixty. In 1890 a single operative in America could make cotton cloth enough to supply 1,500 persons.

The improvements in woollen, iron, and miscellaneous manufacturing had perhaps not been quite as great, but were remarkable notwithstanding. Power and automatic machinery were the order of the day. The Corliss engine got 23 per cent. more heat and energy from a given amount of coal than had ever been obtained before it was invented. Instead of the twenty-five days which the first transatlantic steamer required for the passage from America to England, many vessels now went from New York to Liverpool in considerably less than six days, or at an average rate of more than twenty miles an hour. The speed of passenger trains on the main railways had doubled. So had the weight of the freight-car load and the amount of freight which an engine could pull. The newest loco-motives weighed nearly or quite one hundred tons each.

In 1869 a submarine cable was laid which joined the United States to the continent of Europe. It extended about 3,050 miles, from Duxbury, Mass., to Brest, France, via the Island of St. Pierre, south of Newfoundland. The company owning the cable was chartered by the waning empire of Louis Napoleon. In 1875 a new cable was stretched between the United States and Great Britain. It was called the United States Direct Cable, and at first operated in opposition to the original one. The rates for cable messages were greatly reduced in consequence. The price, once ten dollars a word, fell in anticipation of the competition to fifty cents, and to twenty-five after the competition actually began. The two Anglo-American lines were subsequently united.

Cornelius Vanderbilt.

The year 1869 witnessed the junction of
the Union Pacific with the Central Pacific
Railway, forming a continuous railway line
between the Atlantic and Pacific shores.
The last rail was put down on May 12th,

and on the 15th trains began to run. This work had been in process of construction ever since 1863. It traversed the Rocky Mountain range at an elevation of 8,243 feet above sea-level. The Northern Pacific Railway Company was chartered by Congress in 1864. The road was not completed till August, 1883, nor opened to traffic before September. Its length from Duluth to its then terminus on the Columbia River, Washington, was 1,674 miles. The Southern Pacific and the Atlantic and Pacific, both traversing the Rockies, soon followed. Still another line, the Great Northern, connecting St. Paul with the extreme Northwest, was opened in 1893. The country's total railway mileage in 1885 was 128,967 miles; in 1893 it was 170,607 miles.

In the same years with the opening of these continental lines began the consolidation of the older ones into great systems. The New York Central had already been formed out of sixteen different fragments, but the process of consolidation in a large way may be said to have been instituted by

The Big Loop on the Georgetown Branch of the Union Pacific, Colorado.

Cornelius Vanderbilt in 1869, when he joined the Lake Shore and Michigan Southern with the New York Central, thus placing under a single administration the entire route from New York to Chicago. The

Charles F. Brush.

first train pierced the Hoosac Tunnel, in Western Massachusetts, February 9, 1875, completing another artery between East and West. The tunnel passed through the Hoosac Mountain, a distance of four miles and three-quarters, and had been in process of boring, though not continuously, about fifteen years.

The lighting of large spaces by electricity in a profitable manner may be dated from **1875.** The possibility of producing a bril-

Moses G. Farmer.

liant light with this fluid had been well known to physicists ever since Sir Humphry Davy's experiments in 1813, but no method of generating the electricity cheaply had hitherto been invented. Utilizing

Thomas A. Edison.

among others the inventions of Dr. C. W.
Siemens, Mr. Charles G. Brush, of Cleve-

The Hoosac Tunnel Lit by Glow Lamps, after the Plan of the Marr Construction Company.

land, O., gave to the world in 1875 his re-
markably efficient dynamo or generator, and

from that time the illumination of streets
and squares by electricity began to be somewhat common.   There was, to be sure,
another difficulty to be overcome, even for
lighting on a grand scale, that of maintaining a steady and continuous light.   In this
the Jablochkoff candle, used in the Paris
streets by 1878, was measurably successful.
It was a voltaic arc arrangement, in which,
by making each of the two carbon pencils
alternately positive and negative, their ends
were consumed with equal rapidity and so
kept perpetually the same distance apart.

But the voltaic light was too brilliant for
a small area.   How to divide and subdue
it so as to render it suitable for house lighting, was still a difficult problem.   Farmer,
Sawyer, Mann, and Edison, all attacked it
at nearly the same time, going back with
singular accord from the voltaic arc prin-
ciple to that of incandescence in a vacuum.
Edison, the prodigy of the century in in-
ventive genius, was the most successful.
Besides improving the dynamo, he per-
fected with little difficulty a cheap vacuum-

globe.   After long experimenting he succeeded in the more arduous task of securing
an automatic checking of the current before
it became hot enough to consume the incandescent carbon.   He also found that a

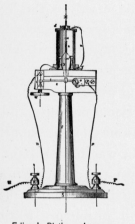

Edison's Platinum Lamp on
Carbon Support, 1879.

Edison's Paper
Carbon Lamp.

large current could be divided into smaller
ones by splitting up the conductor into
minor filaments.   Triumph in household
illumination was thus achieved, and when,
in October, 1878, the results of Edison's
experimenting were announced to the world,
gas fell from twelve to twenty per cent.

The alarm was premature, however, since
the new illumination did not, after all, prove
so satisfactory as to displace the old.   It
largely did so for streets, factories, and halls,
but to no very great extent for residences.

The most stupendous engineering work
yet accomplished by man, the great bridge

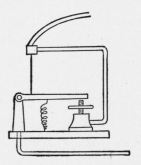

Edison's First Incandescent Platinum Lamp.

spanning East River between Brooklyn and
New York, was completed in May, 1883,
excavations for its foundations having begun so early as 1870.   This wonder of the
world was designed by John A. Roebling,
and after his death in 1869 finished by
his son, W. A. Roebling.   It cost about
$16,000,000, two-thirds coming from the city

of Brooklyn, one-third from New York. A gigantic stone tower, 277 feet high, was built on each side of the river. Through arched apertures in these toward the top ran the roadway, its ends being 119 feet above the water. The centre of the bridge was supported by four steel wire cables, 16 inches in diameter, which passed from solid masonry structures nearly 1,000 feet away from the water's edge on either shore, up over the two towers, dipping, at the centre of the river, to nearly the level of the roadway. On account of their great weight they had to be braided, strand by strand, in their permanent position. Suspenders from these cables grappled the body of the bridge at frequent intervals. The main span was 1,595½ feet long, the entire work about 6,000 feet. There were five passageways—two on the outside for carriages, the next two for cable cars, the middle one for foot passengers. The bridge curved upward from each tower, being at the middle 135 feet above the water in summer, and three feet higher in winter, owing to contraction by the cold. All but the very largest ships sailed under without shortening their masts.

In connection with the great bridge, as likewise in a way possessing an importance for the whole nation, we may mention the ingenious deepening of Hell-gate Channel, East River, by tunnelling beneath the water and using dynamite; and also the introduction of elevated railways in New York City and Brooklyn. This project had been mooted by 1868. Exactly ten years later two sections of railway were open for travel in New York. The first elevated road in Brooklyn began operation in 1885. These new avenues of travel at once became immensely popular. In 1884, no fewer than 250 engines and 800 cars were in use by the New York lines, carrying over 300,000 passengers daily, or about 103,000,000 for the year. Nearly at the same time with the introduction of these roads in New York, new methods of traction for surface street railways, by electricity and by cable, were introduced in various cities of the country,

The Brooklyn Bridge, looking up the East River.

bidding fair soon to do away with horses for
this service.

The Manhattan Elevated Railway, New York.

One of the most interesting and valuable
inventions of this or any century was that

of the telephone, devised by Alexander
Graham Bell, and first put to business use
in 1877. For ten years Mr. Bell had been
experimenting upon the possibility of con-
veying sound by means of the electric wire.
In 1876 he had so far succeeded as to exhibit a pair of his instruments in successful
operation at the Philadelphia Centennial
Exhibition. In April of the next year the
Cambridge Water Board, the Pennsylvania
Railroad, and many other corporations
ordered the instrument for practical service. From this time the business grew
with incredible rapidity. The American
Bell Telephone Company was incorporated,
and in January, 1886, had in use 330,000
telephones. There were this year in
various cities of the United States 752
telephone exchanges. The total length
of telephone wires operated by this company was 114,371 miles. In addition to
the system which centred in the Bell
Company there were several competing
telephone establishments in continual litiga-
tion with the Bell. The total mileage of

telephone wires in the United States in 1887
was estimated at 130,000 miles.   There were
the same year 170,000 miles of telegraph
wire, besides private lines.   In 1893, the
aggregate length of telegraph lines in the

Under Side of a Modern Switchboard, showing 2,000 Telegraph Wires.

United States open to the public exceeded
210,000 miles.   There were, besides, government and private lines to a length vast but
not ascertainable.   In addition to all this,
the Bell Telephone Company, which conducted the main telephone business of the

country, owned, the same year, 307,748 miles of wire, which the lines of other companies increased to 440,750 miles.

From this account of our country's material advance after the war we purposely omit mention of the great economic progress at the South, as that has been already reviewed in Chapter IV. We must, instead, notice several events which decidedly checked the prosperity of these years.

So soon as gold had ceased to circulate in 1862, speculation in it began, which was one of the most pernicious results of the depreciation of paper. The ups and downs in the gold price of the greenback from week to week and from day to day during the war were largely due to this cause. In 1869 a clique of speculators in New York thought to realize an immense fortune by cornering gold, a large proportion of the stock east of the Rocky Mountains being known to be in New York City.

By Wednesday, September 22d, they had pushed up the price of gold in greenbacks

from 131 to 141, causing a disastrous tumble
in stocks and almost a panic.   The money
market grew tight, and interest enormous.
Loans were to be had only on the very

Professor Bell Sending the First Message by Long-distance Telephone,
from New York to Chicago.

best securities.   On Thursday gold still
advanced, showing that the corner remained

The New York Gold Room on "Black Friday," September 24, 1869.

solid.   At the last call it stood at 144;
at the first on Friday, September 24th, 105
was the figure.   The ring was believed at
this time to hold in gold and in contracts

to deliver the same, over $100,000,000, while all the gold in New York outside the United States Sub-Treasury was hardly over $10,000,000. Only the Government could break the corner. At eleven o'clock gold was at 155, whence in half an hour it rose to 160, then to 162, then to 164. In the midst of an excitement never paralleled in the Gold Room before or since, it was announced on authority that the Government would sell. The price at once went down to 135, and the power of the clique was instantly broken. This day passed into history under the name of " Black Friday."

The Chicago fire of October, 1871, was the most disastrous yet in the chronicles of our country. It began in the evening of October 8th and raged for over twenty-four hours. According to the best estimates 250 lives were lost, 98,500 persons made homeless, 17,500 buildings consumed, and $192,000,000 worth of property destroyed. The main business portion of the city was included in the tract burned. Thirteen months later the most destructive conflagration that had ever visited Boston swept the district below Washington Street from Summer nearly to State, and eastward to the water's edge, being the most solid business

A Scene during the Chicago Fire.

portion of the city.   The loss was placed at $75,000,000.

The shocking destruction of wealth by these fires was part cause of the hard times which began in 1873. But others concurred. During 1872 the balance of trade was

strongly against the United States. The
circulation of depreciated paper money had
brought to many an apparent prosperity
which was not real, leading to the free
contraction of debts by individuals, corporations, towns, cities, and States. An unprece-
dented mileage of railways had just been
constructed. During the half decade ending with 1873, $1,700,000,000 had thus been
spent in the country. The supposed wealth
of many consisted in the bonds of these
roads and of other newly created concerns,
as mining and manufacturing corporations.
Thus the entire business of the country was
on a basis of inflation, and when contraction
came by the resumption of specie payments
and the demonetization of silver, disaster
was inevitable.

In the course of the summer solid values
began to be hoarded and interest rates con-
sequently to rise. In September panic came.
Credit in business was refused, debtors were
pressed for payment, securities were rushed
into the market and fell greatly in price,
railway stocks from ten to forty per cent.,

even United States bonds from five to ten.
There was a run upon savings banks, many
of which succumbed.   For ten days, beginning September 20th, the New York Stock
Exchange had to suspend, so dubious was
the value of most stock contracts.   Manu-
factured products were little salable, and
the prices of agricultural painfully sank.
Factories began to run on short time, many
closed entirely, many corporations failed.
The peculiarity of this crisis was the slowness with which it abated.   No date indeed
can be set as its term, its evil effects drag-
ging on through years, so that the ill times
of 1893–94 may be regarded as the same
fever, intermittent in the meantime.

Notwithstanding all these drawbacks, the
material progress of the United States for
the two decades which we are studying was
something enormous.   We have no room
for details.   Our total population by 1880
had swollen to 50,155,783, by 1890 to 62,-
622,250.   The census valuation of our national wealth, which had been for 1860,
$16,159,616,068, was, for 1870, $30,068,518,-

507; for 1880, $43,642,000,000; and for 1890, $65,037,091,197. The *per capita* wealth was, according to the census of 1860, $5.14, by that of 1870, $780, by that of 1880, $870, by that of 1890, $1,036. In 1870 the United States was in wealth the third nation on the globe; in 1880 it had distanced France and stood second. " The country whose population has been developed within two hundred and eighty years, does already one-third of the world's mining, one-fourth of its manufacturing, and one-fifth of its agriculture ; and at least one-sixth of the world's wealth is already concentrated in the strip of territory in Central North America which is the home of the United States." These words were written after the census of 1880. Still stronger ones would have been true in 1895.

CHAPTER IX.

END OF THE PERIOD

IT is a long way that we have taken the reader, from the days of Columbus to where we can espy the dawn of the twentieth century. Yet, in comparison with the times which our narrative has here reached, those of three decades earlier would seem almost as remote as Columbus's own, so swiftly did the wheels of progress turn. Everything declared that a new age had opened. In addition to the signs of this which have been set down in the preceding chapters, we have only space for the bare mention of a few others.

In 1888 the United States mails flew from point to point across the continent with a rapidity which would have astounded people so few years back as the close of the war. Their distribution, effected through the post-office cars that ran on all the main lines, and by immediate delivery in cities and large towns, was quite as great an improvement as the speed. The postal-car system had origin in Chicago in 1864, spreading thence East and West. Speedy delivery was introduced in 1886. Postal rates were lower than ever before, and destined soon to be lower still. Much business formerly left to the express companies was now done by mail, and much carried on in this way which formerly was not done at all.

Our country had developed an attention to art in all its forms far beyond anything of the kind to be observed at the end of the war. In all the principal cities concerts of the highest order were provided and numerously attended. Our art galleries already vied with many of those in the Old World. Students of art were found in abundance in our own multiplying schools for them, while many from this country sought art instruction in Europe. Not a few Americans attained eminence in this department year by year. In one artistic line we already excelled every other people, viz., the application of the principles of taste in beautifying homes, churches, structures intended for business, such as exchanges, railway stations, and bridges, cars, and all kinds of machinery. We led the world, too, in propriety and neatness of apparel, at least, for men.

After the war the right to vote was extended in nearly all the States, until by 1890 manhood suffrage was legally the rule from North to South and from East to West. In this, indeed, we were only keeping pace with Great Britain, France, Italy, Switzerland, and Germany. The agitation for woman's suffrage had, however, progressed further here than in any other land. There was a large party, quasi-political, intent upon bringing it about. A national convention was held in that interest each year. In Wyoming and Utah the suffrage had already been enjoyed by women since 1869. In Kansas, by a law going into effect February 16, 1887, they voted on all municipal affairs.   In many other localities they had the privilege of voting on certain questions, as the election of school committees, and were eligible to membership in these committees.   Occupations of honor and profit were, more and more as the years passed, open to the female sex.   Women preached, practised law and medicine, and furnished many of the best bookkeepers, sales-people, and principals of schools. Vassar College, the first institution in the world for the full collegiate education of women, was opened in 1861.   Smith and Wellesley Colleges, for the same, were opened in 1875, Bryn Mawr following in 1885.   Cornell, Michigan, and all the State Universities in the West, like a number of the best universities in the East, educated young women on the same terms as young men.   Harvard opened its Radcliffe College for female pupils.   At its commencement in 1886, Columbia College, of which the Barnard College for women became virtually a part, conferred the degree of Doctor in Philosophy upon a woman.   Yale

Catching the Mail Pouch from the Crane.

University and the University of Pennsylvania opened their graduate departments to women on the same terms as to men. Brown University did the same, besides providing for the undergraduate instruction of women.

Another sign of the times, still more striking, was our advance toward socialism and state socialism. This occurred for the most part in ways so recondite as to escape observation, yet in many respects the course of things in this direction was perfectly obvious. The powerful movement for the legal prohibition of the manufacture and sale of intoxicants was one instance. The extension and perfection of our public school system, all at the expense of the tax-payers, was another, it being possible by 1890 in nearly every State for a young person of either sex to secure, without paying a cent of tuition money, a better education than the finest universities in the land could give a hundred years previous. The extension of governmental surveillance over great industries was another illustration. The

Trusts spoken of in a preceding chapter were unhesitatingly assumed to be subject to legislative investigation and command. Great corporations and combinations, it was now well understood, could not pursue their ends merely for profit, irrespective of public interest. The Inter-State Railway Law of February 4, 1887, instituting a National Commission, to which all railways crossing state lines were responsible for obedience to certain rules which the same law enjoined, was the boldest assertion of state supervision yet made; but there was a great and growing number of thinkers who believed that mere state oversight would not suffice, and that at least gigantic businesses like telegraph, railway, and mining, must sooner or later be bought and operated out and out by public authority. Nothing had done so much to promote this conviction as the rise, procedure, and wealth of these Trusts, for from the oppressive greed of many of them no legislative regulation seemed sufficient to protect the people.

This tendency to over-exalt the State's industrial function was not the only danger which confronted us. Another was that from immigration. So enormous was the influx of foreigners that we were threatened with a fatal emasculation of our national character. The manner in which we incorporated alien elements theretofore was among the wonders of history, but it was at least a question whether we could continue to do this always. It seemed in part therefore a healthy sentiment which by the law of 1882 excluded Chinese labor-immigrants. New-comers from other lands were also refused domicile here if imported under contract,[1] or unable to support themselves. The stronger law against the Chinese at first sight seemed invidious, but there was some justification for it in the fact that those people almost never settled down permanently as citizens of the United States, but returned to their native land so soon as they earned a competence. Italians of the lowest class did this to some extent,

---

[1] Law of February 26, 1885.

but the great bulk of our foreign-born population came here with the purpose of becoming American.

Our Irish-American fellow-citizens gave
concern to many. One complaint was that
they brought hither their anti-English
prejudices, by the loud and continual assertion of which they tended ever to embroil
us with England. There proved to be
slight danger from this source, particularly
after the rise of a powerful pro-Irish sentiment and party among the English themselves. Others had great fear of the Irish
as Catholics, they being the chief representatives of that faith in the United States.
The growth of the Roman Catholic Church
in our borders was certainly very rapid.
An American clergyman, McCloskey, was
made Cardinal in 1875. A University,
subject to the Catholic Church was
erected in Washington. Catholicism in
America was no longer a mission church as
it had been until quite recently, but had a
full national organization as in the other
great nations of the earth.

A strong movement was developed among the Catholic clergy against our common schools as usually administered. Parochial schools were erected in most Eastern cities and large towns, and efforts made to fill them with children who, but for their existence, would be in the public schools. Public schools were denounced as godless because they did not, as of course they could not, give positive religious instruction. This opposition was doubtless a menace to our time-honored and on the whole very efficient school system, so that what the future of this was to be no one could confidently predict. It was to be remarked, however, that some of the warmest defenders of the public schools appeared in the Catholic ranks ; nor was there any evidence that, as a class, American citizens of Irish birth and descent prized the free institutions of this nation a whit less than the rest of the people.

A greater peril beset the nation in the decay which slowly crept over our family life. The family has in every civilized age been justly regarded as the pillar of the state, but the integrity which it possessed among our fathers, their children invaded in many ways. Mormonism, decadent if not dead, about which so much had been said, was but one of these, and perhaps not the worst. If crimes of a violent nature were becoming less frequent, crimes against chastity were on the increase. Easy divorce was considerably responsible for this. The diversity of marriage and divorce laws in the various States was a great abomination. How to remedy it did not appear. Many called for a constitutional amendment, lodging solely in Congress the power of making laws upon this vital subject.

We proved very fortunate as a people in that our material prosperity itself did not prove a greater curse. More than every other disaster was to be feared the growth of a temper for mere material thinking and enjoyment, the love of lucre and of those merely material comforts and delights which lucre can buy. There was among us quite too little care for the ideal side of life. Too many who purchased books loved them only for the money they cost. Rich engravings and bindings were often sought rather than edifying matter. Costly daubs were purchased at enormous prices for lack of true artistic taste or relish. In sadly frequent cases the great captain of industry was nothing but a plodder. There was too great rush for wealth. We became nervous. Nervous diseases increased alarmingly. We read, but only market reports. Think, we did not ; we only reckoned.

The outlook, notwithstanding, embraced much that was hopeful. Very worthful as well as very beautiful was the new sense of nationality that had been developed in this country in consequence of the war. While men still differed as to the original nature of our Union, while the State remained as yet a vital though a decreasingly important organ of the political frame, its real status offering to reward study as never before because no longer a sectional issue, yet the war, as unmistakably pronouncing the national will, laid the question of Nation's supremacy

over State forever at rest, having here-
upon virtually the effect of a constitutional
amendment.   Close construction of the
Constitution could never again throttle this
Union.   Whether such quasi-amendment

Igloos, or Esquimau Huts.

altered the Constitution, Stephens's view,
or served but to bring out more clearly its
old meaning, our view, practically the war
had entailed enormous new exaltation and
centralization of the Union, with answering
subordination of the State.

A. W. Greely.

A quickened sense of our duty as a nation might likewise be observed at work in various directions. Our treatment of the Indians had been, since the administration of President Grant, more humane than ever before. Earnest and successful efforts were made, very largely at the national expense, to educate them and prepare them for citizenship. They were better protected from the rapacity of heartless agents and frontiersmen, while the land in severalty legislation of 1887 opened the red man's way to the actual attainment of civil rights and to all the advance in civilization of which he was capable.

The part which our Government had begun to take in the advancement of science was greatly to its credit. We have space to instance only the expedition of 1881–1884, headed by Lieutenant Greely, to the northern polar regions for scientific observation, reaching a point nearer to the pole than had ever before been attained. The whole world admired the daring and sympathized with the sufferings of these gallant explorers, several of whom perished of cold and hunger before relief reached them, the others rescued barely in season to save them from like fate.

The revision of King James's version of our English Bible, New Testament finished in 1881, Old Testament in 1885, was an eminent historical event falling in this period. American divines took prominent part in it, though of course not under any commission from our Government.

Being the most trying crisis ever successfully met by a self-governed people, the war lent powerful stimulus and tonic to the cause of free institutions everywhere, proving republican loyalty to be as firm and trustworthy as monarchical, and government by and for the governed to be not necessarily either inefficient or ephemeral. It demonstrated that a republic, without lessening its freedom, may become a great military power, generals of highest genius passively obeying a popularly elected Congress and Executive, these in turn maintaining full mastery, yet not hampering military movements.

The achievement of this firmer national unity, with the success and the martial and financial prodigies attending the struggle therefor, gave us new and far higher place in the esteem of nations, with correspondingly enlarged influence in mankind's greater affairs.

By 1890 one might observe a more or less conscious disposition on the part of thoughtful Americans to insist that this influence be exerted, to have the nation break over the policy wisely laid down by Washington, for earlier times, and assert itself more in the Parliament of Man. It was felt that our place and power among the nations of the earth had not been given us for naught, and that, as the weal of mankind is to a considerable degree determined by international politics, we had no right longer to hold ourselves aloof from this field. The feeling was emphasized by the annihilation of space between us and other nations, brought about through steam navigation and ocean telegraphy.

Not only Great Britain and France, but Germany, Russia, and China were now at our very doors.　They would influence our weal whether or not we reacted upon them. Why should we not, without being meddlesome, strive to disseminate our ideas, extend our civilization, and make our national personality felt?　It was to President Arthur's praise that he caused the United States to be represented at Berlin in the Congo Conference of 1884–85.　Next, men said, our delegates would be present with voice and vote in all regular Congresses of the Great Powers.　Americans did not prophesy, as more than one voice out of Europe itself had of late done, that the United States would some day cross the Atlantic as a conqueror.　This, indeed, was a somewhat natural thought.　The Old World reeled under its crushing burden of national debts and military taxes, and in material resources could not long compete with us, free from such burdens. But the American thought was that we should express our superiority in the form of ideas, not of arms, and use it in elevating mankind to richer culture and a nobler life.